Nothing but a Circus

Misadventures among the Powerful

DANIEL LEVIN

ALLEN LANE
an imprint of
PENGUIN BOOKS

ALLEN LANE

UK | USA | Canada | Ireland | Australia
India | New Zealand | South Africa

Allen Lane is part of the Penguin Random House group of companies whose
addresses can be found at global.penguinrandomhouse.com

First published 2017

001

Copyright © Daniel Levin, 2017

The moral right of the author has been asserted

Set in 12/14.75 pt Dante MT Std
Typeset in India by Thomson Digital Pvt Ltd, Noida, Delhi
Printed in Great Britain by Clays Ltd, St Ives plc

A CIP catalogue record for this book is available from the British Library

HARDBACK ISBN: 978–0–241–28853–5
TRADE PAPERBACK ISBN: 978–0–241–29971–5

www.greenpenguin.co.uk

MIX
Paper from
responsible sources
FSC® C018179

Penguin Random House is committed to a
sustainable future for our business, our readers
and our planet. This book is made from Forest
Stewardship Council® certified paper.

For Laura, Noa and Ben
who are doing everything they can to keep me
from turning into one of those characters I tell them about

Contents

Introduction

Over the past twenty years I have laughed a lot and I have cried a lot. But mostly I have laughed a lot. I have met countless experts offering solutions without a problem, countless pundits drawing distinctions without a difference, countless gatekeepers whose only purpose is to make sure that the gates they are guarding remain closed, and countless political operators fuelled solely by their naked ambition – creatures who will do absolutely nothing, no matter how worthy the cause, if it does not advance their careers. I have witnessed many grandiose politicians take responsibility for their mistakes with bombastic displays of contrition, without really taking responsibility for their mistakes because they got others to pay the price and take the fall. I have met rulers who are pure geniuses when it comes to accumulating and preserving power, but when it comes to governing – not so much. During these years I have perfected my passage through all the saturated stages of failure: from rejection to denial, from denial to disappointment, from disappointment to disbelief, from disbelief to irritation, from irritation to outrage, from outrage to anger, from anger to contempt, and from contempt to resignation. And then I went through the same cycle over and over again, learning nothing from my mistakes other than the fact that I learn nothing from my mistakes.

The craziest part about these stories is that they are all true. They occurred during the past two decades in the course of my travels all over the globe. My own involvement in these episodes tended to be more incidental than fundamental, more that of a spectator than of a protagonist, in many different roles and circumstances – as a lawyer in emerging markets advising on privatizations or country debt restructurings, trying to implement financial literacy and political inclusion initiatives, or attempting to mediate between belligerent parties in conflict zones. I found myself in the wild and bizarre situations recounted in the following chapters not as a result of some grand professional strategy or splendid career plan, but rather as an eyewitness reeling from one mind-boggling experience to another.

My earliest memories go back to my childhood in East Africa in the 1960s, at a time when the continent was brimming with post-independence promise and aspirations. The pristine innocence and happiness of those years have continued to define the paradise of my dreams. Perhaps it was the quest to rediscover that paradise that caused me to keep coming back to Africa as an adult, though it is just as plausible that a childhood on the move made me as rooted – or lost – in Africa as in the Middle East, Europe, North America, or Asia. Multiple roots equal no roots – too many new beginnings, too many departures without goodbyes. Perhaps it was the illusory comparison to the lost bliss of my childhood that made me question why those in power so rarely used this power to raise those below them. I wondered – maybe just as illusorily – whether it was possible to do things a little differently, if not to reverse the downward trajectory of many countries, then at least to slow the pace at which things seemed to be falling apart. In the course of my work I witnessed the disastrous ineffectiveness of multilateral institutions, aid agencies, and prominent consultancies, which seemed organizationally inept and unwilling to rethink their palpably flawed approach to development. And eventually, by the time I had become disillusioned and cynical myself after years in which each moment of success and elation hoodwinked me into muffling and ignoring my many moments of failure and disappointment, perhaps it was just a sense of dejection and deadly boredom that led me to defy my own beliefs and assumptions; a boredom caused by overexposure to cloned, copy-paste advisory mandates that ended up as boilerplate diagnostic reports rife with platitudes and, for the few that were actually implemented, as cannibalized initiatives that imported and compounded the mistakes and shortcomings of previous projects. I cannot say for sure. What I do know is that I benefited from humbling, sometimes painful experiences that taught me how little I really knew, and how much more those I was purporting to teach knew and understood. These were the experiences that spurred me on to create a development platform that could tackle challenges such as financial literacy, political and financial inclusion, public education, and capacity building a little differently, with less conventional methods, focused less on telling others what to do, and more on providing them with the know-how and the tools to tailor and implement their own reforms based on their own political, economic, social, religious, and cultural realities. Only after my partners and I had changed our methodology and developed this platform for the people on the ground, and only after we had figured out that we could never get callous rulers to do the right thing unless we also convinced them that doing the right thing would make them appear as immortal saviours of the human race – doing good and doing well at the same time – only then did we start to experience some success, and only then did my work in Africa feel less like a visit and more like a return home.

Throughout these two decades of interacting with a few great people and with many people claiming to be great, I had to navigate corridors of power, and in the process I became fairly nimble in handling the jesters and eunuchs who roam and control these courts. I did expect to encounter self-importance and self-aggrandizement, vanity and narcissism. I did expect to meet backstabbers and tools, self-aggrandizers and fabricators. I did expect to face incompetence and ineptitude. I was not disappointed. What I did not expect, however, is for people in and around power to be so predictable, and so extraordinarily ordinary. Perhaps I just happened to meet the wrong people, or perhaps, as my friend Ayanda once told me, it's because the good ones usually die young.

With increasing success and power, it takes less for the means to justify the ends, and for the ends to justify the means. Nowhere is the blurring of the lines between means and ends more prevalent than in politics. A new type of conscience emerges – no longer an inner voice that distinguishes between right and wrong, but instead one of continuous validation and justification of self-serving choices. My own fascination lies with the moment at which this transition takes form, and the contortions that raw ambition and careerism can demand in order to maintain the illusion of integrity, decency, and public service.

As I said, all the following events and conversations did take place. There was no need to fictionalize these episodes – reality proved to be stranger and funnier than fiction. I did, however, change some of the names and chronologies or otherwise anonymize the individuals involved, because it was not my goal to shame or expose any particular person, or to settle any scores. My aim was to show the all too human underbelly of the people who inhabit these bubbles, and to celebrate the memories with a twinkle and a smile.

Prologue

The phone rang a few minutes after midnight.

'I hope I'm not disturbing you.' It took me a moment to figure out who was calling me at such a late hour.

'Not at all, Mary,' I lied. 'What can I do for you?'

'I'm looking for Mr Grant. His wife and son have been in a terrible car accident, and I can't find him. Do you have any idea where he might be?'

Mark Grant was the partner I worked for almost exclusively at one of the major Wall Street law firms in New York. I had met Mark when he came to speak to foreign law students at Columbia University on a Friday afternoon, and we soon found ourselves immersed in a conversation about the cultural differences between practising law in America and in Europe. Since Mark had grown up in Germany before coming to the US after law school for a master's degree, he could easily relate to my background and my worries about being able to find my professional footing in New York. He invited me for an interview at his law firm, and I ended up being offered a position based largely on Mark's generous recommendation and high standing in the firm. For the past three years I had spent more time talking to him than to any other person, possibly even more than to all other persons combined. We worked together around the clock, and our interaction extended to all hours of the night and to weekends. Mark was a workaholic on steroids. The incessant work was Mark's raison d'être, his identity. Sadly, this had become my life, too. One transaction after another, endless drafting of agreements and acrimonious negotiations, myriad legal opinions. During my first year attached to Mark at the hip, I had billed 4,160 hours. Eighty hours a week! Billed. Which means I practically lived at the office, and most of the time that I was there, Mark was there, too.

I knew that Mark was in Europe, but I had not spoken to him that day. Every once in a while, he had a tendency to disappear, and I usually had little incentive to forgo a rare moment of peace from my obsessive boss.

'My goodness!' I said. 'No, Mary, I haven't heard from him today. Did you try the Frankfurt office?'

'I did, and also his apartment in Frankfurt. He is not there. Please, Daniel, could you try to find him and ask him to call me immediately?'

I realized that I hadn't yet asked about the accident. 'What happened to his wife and son? Are they okay?'

'Sort of,' said Mary. 'The car flipped on the Taconic Parkway. Hillary was driving and must have lost control. She fractured some vertebrae in her neck, but Matt wasn't hurt. The dog was thrown out of the car, but it seems that he wasn't hurt either.'

'That's terrible. Will Hillary make a full recovery?' I said.

'The doctors say she will be fine, eventually. She was lucky. She could have easily been paralysed. The whole thing could have been much worse. But I need to reach Mr Grant, so that he can come home immediately. I booked him on the fastest flight home tomorrow, with the Concorde via London.'

'Don't his wife and kids have a way to reach him?'

'I asked them. They have no idea where he is nor how to reach him. They didn't even know that he was in Europe. You're probably the person he's the closest to.'

I promised Mary to do everything I could to find Mark and to call her as soon as I did.

Mary had been Mark's secretary for many years. She was about his age – early sixties – and could have retired long ago, but she was fully devoted to him. Still, I detected a whiff of annoyance in her voice. It irritated her that Mark was unreachable in Europe, while his wife was lying in a hospital bed in New York with a serious injury.

I never made it to bed that night. I spent the next six hours calling every person who might have had any contact with Mark in Frankfurt or in the firm's Düsseldorf office. I spoke to them all – his German secretary, the partners and associates, the legal assistants, the receptionists, his regular driver, even his elderly Greek housekeeper. None of them had any idea where he was or how to reach him. Mark didn't believe in cell phones, which at the time had not yet become as ubiquitous as they are today. Perhaps because it was the only way for him to carve out some undisturbed private hours for himself or, more likely, because he just couldn't be bothered to carry one around.

During the long hours that night my mind wandered back to memories of the places all over the world Mark and I had visited together. I had particularly fond memories of our experiences together in South Africa at a time when the country was dancing with joy and hopefulness just weeks after Nelson Mandela's presidential inauguration. I remembered the time out we took from our work in Cape Town to hike up Table Mountain and experience the most beautiful sunset, as well as our drive to the Cape of Good Hope and Cape Point, near the area where the Atlantic and the Indian oceans meet. I had never seen Mark laugh as much as when two large baboons sat on the hood of our car, stared at us, and refused to leave. On that trip I had introduced Mark to my good friends Eli and Yasmin Long. Eli was a South African diplomat, and he graciously agreed to introduce our law firm to some of the largest South African companies and several government ministers. Eli even helped us organize a seminar, in which Mark and several of the firm's partners spoke to South African officials about the US capital markets. Unfortunately, their presentations were so dull and uninspiring that the whole event backfired. Even Eli, who was generally so courteous and tactful, remarked that he had come to the seminar expecting an interesting lecture, and instead had received a sedative. I had had such high expectations for this seminar, hoping that it would launch the law firm in South Africa and beyond on the continent. Instead, I realized that Mark and his partners lacked the curiosity and the humility to relate to other cultures. That evening I wondered for the first time whether I might be better off on my own, if I wanted to do meaningful work in Africa.

I finally reached Mark in his Frankfurt apartment eighteen hours later around midnight on Sunday, Frankfurt time. He picked up in a splendid, energized mood, and was not the least bit annoyed by my midnight phone call.

'Oh hello, Daniel. Nice to hear from you. Have you been able to finish the prospectus for our favourite client?'

No foreplay, just work. Par for the course.

I apologized for calling him at such a late hour and informed him, as gently as I could, of the car accident and his wife's fractured neck vertebrae.

'Very sorry to hear that,' Mark said in a perfectly calm voice. 'Glad Matt is fine. Shall we talk in the morning and go over a few points in the documents you sent me on Friday?'

I was perplexed. I assumed Mark was in shock and denial, so I started to explain all over again what had happened, softly and slowly, but he cut me off after a few words.

'I understood you the first time, Daniel,' he said impatiently. 'I will be back in New York at the end of the week and will deal with it then.'

My reaction migrated quickly from empathy to disdain, accelerated by Mark's snippiness. 'Mark, your wife is lying in a hospital with a broken neck, which will require surgery that is not without risk. I really think you should fly back as soon as you can. Mary booked you on the first plane in the morning.'

A pause. 'Oh, I see,' Mark said, sounding uninterested. 'You know, Daniel, I have this important meeting with our favourite client on Thursday. I really think it would be unwise to cancel it. What do you think?'

'What do I think? What do you think I think?' It came out a little harsher than intended. Evidently, the thought of rushing home to be by the side of his wife of thirty-two years had not crossed his mind. 'I think you should come back immediately. Call Dr Maus and explain why you have to postpone the meeting, or, if you want, I can do that for you. I have no doubt he'll understand.'

Well, the meeting was never cancelled. Mark showed up for the appointment with Dr Maus and his colleagues on Thursday afternoon in Frankfurt, and returned to New York on Friday evening. I was sitting at my desk at the office when he waltzed in straight from the airport, not a worry in the world, and proceeded to tell me how well the meeting with Dr Maus had gone.

This time, it was my turn to interrupt. 'Mark, just a thought, but you might want to consider checking in on Hillary at the hospital. The swelling in her neck is down, and the doctors have scheduled the surgery for tomorrow morning. I'm sure she'll be quite pleased to see you. It will be a nice surprise.' I had not meant to sound so sardonic, but I did not need to worry, as my sarcasm was completely lost on him.

'You're probably right,' Mark said. 'I'll ask Mary to get me a car, and I'll head over there soon.'

Soon. Not right away. Not five days ago. At that moment I knew that I was at the wrong place. It was time to leave.

PART ONE

Charmed in Big Sandy

Shortly after freeing myself from Mark Grant's embrace, I took the plunge and, together with my friend Gregg, set up shop across town in our own law firm. Luckily, we hit the ground running, and within a few days we had more work than we could handle. But as grateful as I was for all the legal mandates, they were all domestic American transactions. What I really coveted was interesting work in Africa.

Just two weeks after launching our firm, we were in the midst of planning the opening party for our families, friends, and clients, when it seemed that my prayers had been answered.

'I have a Mr Muture on the line for you,' my secretary said. 'Strong accent, not American.'

I was eager to hear what this person wanted and picked up immediately.

'Good morning,' the gentleman said in a deep and pleasant voice. 'Richard Muture speaking. I received your contact details from a common friend in South Africa, Dr Eli Long.'

His accent sounded Zambian, or perhaps from Botswana or Zimbabwe. I had not spoken to Eli Long since the seminar fiasco with Mark Grant and his partners in South Africa, and I resolved to get in touch with him soon.

'Oh yes, dear Eli,' I replied. 'How is my friend?'

'Eli is doing fabulously well for himself. He left government and now works for the largest insurance company in the country. He is a gem of a human being.'

'He sure is,' I said. 'What can I do for you, Mr Muture?'

'Please, Daniel, call me Richard.'

'Very well, Richard, how can I be of help?'

'Well, Daniel, we have an interesting situation at hand, which I would like to share with you, if you don't mind.'

'Of course,' I said. 'I am all ears.'

'Have you ever heard of Ambassador University or Ambassador College?' Richard asked.

'I'm afraid not,' I answered.

'Ambassador University is . . . Actually, let me start from the beginning, if you don't mind,' Richard said.

'Please do.' I was not sure what to make of this fellow. Something about his over-familiarity seemed a little strange and off-putting, but since I thought highly of Eli, who had made the introduction, I decided to hear him out.

'Thank you, Daniel. Our friend Eli told me that you are an excellent lawyer, and that you are focused on providing financial education and capacity building in Africa. Is that correct?' Richard asked.

'Yes, loosely speaking, that's correct,' I replied. 'At least the Africa-focus part.'

'Well, in that case, it is most opportune that we are talking. My group and I plan to bring young African professionals to America for training. We are thinking about a six-month programme. The training will take place at Ambassador University in East Texas, which we are in the process of acquiring. The university, that is, not East Texas,' he added with a hearty laugh.

'That is very interesting, Richard,' I said. 'How do I fit in?'

'Daniel, what I would really like is for you and your firm to take over the education programme, to train these young people and turn them into future leaders. We will start with a group of fifteen people from my native Zimbabwe. I'm thinking long term, planning ahead for decades to come. This can make a difference in Africa, and perhaps beyond. What do you think, Daniel, do you want to be part of this? Are you interested?'

I was stunned. If someone had asked me to describe the ideal scenario for our firm, Richard Muture's proposal would have come uncannily close to my description. It had everything I could have hoped for – a sustainable education platform, moulding a young generation into future leaders, a dedicated academic institution, and an African focus. I did not have to consider my reply for very long.

'I am very interested, Richard,' I said. 'This sounds like an outstanding project. But I have a few questions. For this to work, everyone needs to be on the same page.'

'You are absolutely right, Daniel,' Richard replied. 'I can assure you that we have a very motivated group behind this, a group with an almost prophetic, divine vision, dare I say. You need to meet everyone. Time is of the essence. We want to get started in the very near future. How soon can you fly to Dallas, Texas?'

'Let me talk to my partner Gregg and get back to you,' I answered.

'Of course,' Richard said. 'But don't wait too long. We are looking at several firms. You would be my first choice, but we do not have the luxury of waiting.'

'I understand,' I said. 'You can expect to hear from me very soon.'

I hung up and walked to Gregg's office. Both of us were swamped closing several transactions, and could ill afford to be out of the office for too long. At the same time, Richard Muture's initiative was too good to pass up. Gregg agreed. As I had to fly abroad the following week, the only real possibility of meeting this group soon was the next day. Even though that risked the appearance of over-eagerness, I hoped that Richard would instead take it as an expression of our enthusiasm and willingness to accommodate his sense of urgency.

I called Richard and told him that Gregg and I could fly to Texas the next morning and spend the day with him and his associates. Richard was thrilled and sounded giddy when describing the exact kerbside location just outside the airport terminal where he and his partner would pick us up.

We found a flight that would leave Newark a little after six in the morning and arrive in Dallas by nine thirty. Gregg and I knew that this meant having to pull an all-nighter at work, and rushing home just to shower and change, before heading out to the airport around four in the morning. But we were too excited about this incredible opportunity to worry about sleep.

We landed in Dallas just before ten and rushed out of the plane. As we walked out of the terminal building, I immediately spotted Richard and his partner standing in front of a green minivan. They were hard to miss – Richard was short and wiry, dressed in a brown pinstripe suit with a pinkish shirt and a bright green tie, while his partner was an enormous man in jeans, cowboy boots, a short-sleeve shirt, and a large white Stetson hat. A tiny African next to a giant redneck, just as Richard had put it.

'Gentlemen, welcome to Texas!' Richard shouted, as he walked towards us with open arms. 'Meet my partner Kyle.'

We all shook hands, and I introduced Richard to Gregg.

'Shall we?' Richard said, gesturing towards the vehicle.

Gregg sat up front in the passenger seat next to Kyle, while I moved to the back with Richard.

'Where are we going?' I asked Richard as we left the airport.

'Daniel, you are about to experience the charm of Big Sandy, Texas,' Richard answered.

'Big Sandy? Where's that?' I asked.

'Big Sandy is about two hours from here, depending on traffic, in the direction of Louisiana,' Kyle said without turning around.

'What's in Big Sandy?' I wanted to know.

'Big Sandy is where Ambassador University is,' Richard replied.

I remembered that he had mentioned Ambassador University during our first phone call. I had forgotten all about it, and now I regretted not knowing more about this institution. I tried to engage Richard about the university and the planned project, but he made it clear he would prefer to talk about all that once we reached our destination. With one ear, I was listening to the small talk between Gregg and Kyle in the front of the car, which seemed to be taking some strange twists. Kyle spoke with a very heavy southern accent, and I had a hard time understanding him.

'So, Gregg,' I heard Kyle ask, 'what do you do for a living?'

'I'm an attorney,' Gregg answered.

'A what?' Kyle asked.

'An attorney. A lawyer,' Gregg clarified.

'Oh, a lawyer,' Kyle said in exaggerated relief, as if that was far preferable to being an attorney.

'And what do you do, Kyle, if I may ask?' Gregg wanted to know.

'I'm in the oil business,' Kyle replied.

'What exactly do you do in the oil business?' Gregg asked.

'I find oil wells,' said Kyle.

'Oh, interesting. And how do you find them?'

'God shows me the way.'

'Oh really?'

'Yes, really. God takes me straight to the wells.'

Gregg turned around and looked at me with an expression that combined disbelief and reproach. All I could muster was an embarrassed smile, and after quietly shaking his head, Gregg turned back to face Kyle.

'And why does God pick you?' Gregg asked.

'Because he loves me, he respects my faith, and he believes in our good pastor Richard,' came Kyle's reply.

I looked at Richard. 'You are a pastor?'

'I have my flock, yes,' Richard said, his voice slightly lower than before. 'But I don't like to brag. Kyle is among my most devoted sheep. And he has been richly rewarded for it.'

It began to dawn on me that this day would turn out to be very different from what I had expected. There was not much I could do about it that very moment, stuck in a minivan on the way to East Texas, so I decided to enjoy the journey as much as possible. Traffic was thinning out, and Kyle was zipping along. We finally arrived in Big Sandy.

Next to the small 'Welcome to Big Sandy' sign at the town entrance, there was a much larger billboard for Ambassador College, with the words 'Worldwide Church of God' just below it. Gregg turned around again and looked at me with a faint smile.

As we pulled up to the main office building, a man in his forties with a deep orange suntan stepped out and walked towards us, beaming with a wide grin.

'Welcome to Ambassador College, welcome to Big Sandy. It's a pleasure to have you here. I'm Ned.'

Richard introduced Gregg and me to Ned. 'These gentlemen have come all the way from New York to help us.'

Before I could say anything, Ned gave us both a big hug. 'Thank you so much, you have no idea how much your visit means to us.'

Gregg gave me another look. The faint smile was gone.

'You boys must be hungry,' Ned said. 'Why don't we step inside and break bread. We have prepared a modest meal.'

Ned walked us to the dining room, where the table was all set for lunch, and introduced us to his assistant Savannah.

'Let us say grace,' Ned said, and added, looking at Richard: 'Reverend, would you be kind enough to lead us?'

Before I knew it, Savannah was holding my left hand, and Richard my right one.

Richard spoke: 'Bless this food to our bodies, and let us hold You in our hearts, O Lord. And bless these two men who have come here today to help us do Your work. Amen.'

The expectation gap between the Big Sandy group and us was reflected in the expression on Gregg's face, which could charitably be described as befuddled. The atmosphere in that dining room was awkward and tense, and I decided to grab the bull by the horns.

'Thank you for your warm reception,' I started cautiously. 'Please forgive me – I hate to put a damper on everyone's good mood – but I'm a little confused about the reason we're here today. I'd be very grateful, and I believe I also speak for Gregg, if one of you could shed a little more light on the purpose of our meeting.' I had spoken the last words while looking at Richard, who was not making eye contact with me.

'Ned, why don't you take it from here?' Richard said.

'Happy to oblige,' Ned said, all frisky. 'As I am sure Richard has told you, Ambassador College has had its challenges in recent years.'

'Actually, Richard has not shared that with me,' I interjected.

'That's good to hear,' Ned continued, completely ignoring my words. 'As you can certainly imagine, I was delighted to learn that you and your clients can fund the acquisition of Ambassador College.'

I was stupefied. 'Can you repeat that, please?'

'Yes, certainly, we were indeed delighted, elated,' Ned carried on without picking up on my obvious dismay.

'Please, Ned,' I said a little louder, 'I would really appreciate if you could start from the beginning. Who is buying Ambassador College, and who is selling it? I'm afraid we are missing some key pieces of information.'

'Yeah, like what the hell we are doing here,' I heard Gregg mumble under his breath.

'Oh, of course, why didn't you say so?' Ned replied. He had either not heard Gregg, or he was artfully ignoring him. 'Where would you like me to begin?'

'Let's start with the basics,' I said. 'Who is selling Ambassador College, who is buying it, and what role do you believe we can play in all this?'

'How familiar are you with the Worldwide Church of God?' Ned asked.

'Not very familiar,' I replied. 'In fact, my knowledge is limited to the billboard I saw at the entrance to this town.'

Ned gave me this pitying look, feeling sorry for me because I had lived my life in such appalling ignorance.

'Well, I will leave your edification on the Church of God to our dear pastor Richard,' Ned said. 'Perhaps he can fill you in later.'

'That would be nice,' I said, looking at Richard, who was still stubbornly refusing to make eye contact.

'Anyway,' Ned continued, 'the Worldwide Church of God owns Ambassador College. It has two other campuses – one in California, and one in England. The Church of God has decided to close this Big Sandy campus.'

Ned paused and looked at Richard and Kyle, as if inviting them to join the conversation. Kyle was busy eating, and judging by Richard's complete lack of reaction, this was not going to happen.

'Okay, and how do we fit in?' I asked, breaking the awkward silence around the table.

'You, your partners, and your clients will fund our group's acquisition of Ambassador College, God willing,' Ned said with a smile.

I tried not to look at Gregg, so that we would both not burst out laughing.

'I'm sorry, but there might be a slight misunderstanding,' I said. 'This is the first I hear about this. Just for the sake of curiosity, hypothetically speaking, how would we help your group fund the purchase of the university? And, more to the point, *why* would we do that?'

'Why? Because you do God's work, just as we do,' Ned replied. 'Richard has great plans for this place. We will bring poor children from Africa, dress them, feed them, educate them, and teach them God's way. It is a holy mission.'

I looked at Richard, and this time I was determined not to look away until he reacted.

Richard looked visibly uncomfortable. 'Ned speaks for us all,' he mumbled meekly.

'Well, then, Ned, since you speak for y'all,' I said, in a failed attempt at a southern accent, 'I hate to disappoint you, but all this sounded a little different when I spoke to Richard.'

Ned didn't miss a beat. 'That is water under the bridge, Daniel. Let's not dwell on the past. Let's instead focus on the future. Let's do what we can to save these poor African souls.'

'Amen,' Kyle mumbled, his mouth full of food.

'Look, Ned,' I said, 'I hate to be the harbinger of bad news. But all this bears no resemblance to what Richard and I discussed by phone. Had I known that this was what you were expecting, we would have never flown down here. We have neither the interest nor the ability to help you fund this thing. We are not in the business of buying universities.'

'Don't say that, Daniel, don't speak without reflection,' Ned said patronizingly. 'Consider this carefully. This is your shot at redemption, at doing God's work.'

'Oh boy,' I heard Gregg mumble.

'I'll try to say this in the nicest way possible, Ned,' I said, trying hard not to lose my temper. 'There are many ways to do God's work. This one is not my first choice. It's also not my second or third choice. In fact, it doesn't make my top fifty.'

'Are you sure?' Ned asked, attempting to save my lost soul one last time.

I was tempted to say 'Pretty goddamn sure,' but instead just answered 'Very sure.'

Ned fell silent for a few moments. The only sound came from Kyle eating. No tension in the room was going to get between this big boy and his meal.

'Fair enough, Daniel,' Ned finally said, perfectly chipper. 'What separates us humans from animals is that God gave us freedom of choice. So I, for one, certainly respect your choice.'

'Too kind.'

'Of course,' he added, 'even when you are misguided. Thankfully, the Merciful One also gave me, gave us, the power to forgive.'

He just could not help himself. I decided to let it go. At this particular moment, I was more concerned with Gregg finding the power in *his* merciful heart to forgive me.

We spent the rest of the meal chatting about sports – Kyle was a huge Dallas Cowboys fan, Gregg rooted for the Detroit Lions – and ended on a pleasant note, as if we were all just a group of old friends catching up over lunch. Before we headed back for Dallas, Ned insisted on giving us an extended tour of the campus of Ambassador College, perhaps in the hope that we would change our minds once we had experienced the celestial magic of the place.

We spent the next hour driving around the totally abandoned campus, which felt like a ghost town. We did not encounter one single person during the entire tour. Our hosts showed us the dormitories, the gym, the library, the main auditorium, even a small airstrip, the cracked runway covered in weeds.

'What is that for?' I asked.

'Foreign dignitaries used to visit us here from time to time,' Ned said. 'They land here, and they like the direct access to the campus.

The last visitor of note was the leader of Israel's Likud Party. Have you ever heard of it?'

'I believe I have,' I replied. 'What was he doing here?'

'The Church of God is very supportive of the Israeli settler movement in Judea and Samaria,' Ned answered, using the biblical terms for the occupied territories in the West Bank. 'We are all God's children, as you know, and we are all equal. But perhaps some are a little more equal than others, you know. In the sense of righteous, you know.'

'Of course,' I said. 'Even when they are misguided.'

We made our way back to the main office building. Ned and Savannah got out of the van.

'It was a pleasure meeting you,' Ned said. 'Have a safe trip back home. And, who knows, perhaps we will meet again.'

'Perhaps, who knows,' I replied. 'Maybe in the next life.' I was not sure how the Worldwide Church of God felt about reincarnation.

The drive back to Dallas was uneventful. Not a word was mentioned about the bizarre meeting in Big Sandy. I did not confront Richard. There was clearly no point. He had tried to get me there in the hope that I would be dazzled by Ambassador College and the prospects of eternal rewards in heaven. It did not quite work out for Richard, and by the look on his face he felt worse than I did.

As we approached Dallas, Kyle turned around and asked: 'I'm getting kind of hungry. Would you boys care to stop somewhere for an early dinner before your flight?'

'No thanks,' Gregg and I blurted out in unison.

Kyle and Richard dropped us off at the airport. Gregg and I left the car and took off, almost running. Once we were in the terminal, we stopped and burst out laughing.

We found a bar and ordered some drinks.

'To Ambassador University and the Church of God,' Gregg said, as we clinked our glasses.

'I'll drink to that!'

The Scotch tasted good. Sinfully good.

Dubai Dreams

It took me weeks after the Big Sandy extravaganza to come to terms with my own gullibility, and every time my memories of this embarrassing day were thankfully about to fade, Gregg would dispense some playful ribbing to remind me of my impressive business development skills and ability to read people using my finely tuned charlatan-radar. I deserved it.

As the Big Sandy jokes receded, I shared the events of that day with my dear friend Jacques, who thought I had got off cheap in learning what deceit and trickery looked like – assuming, of course, I had actually learned my lesson. Jacques was an electrifying figure, small in stature but larger than life. After befriending the Venezuelan petroleum minister over night-time drinks at a hotel bar in Burma in the early 1950s, Jacques had moved to Venezuela and amassed a fortune in steel and banking, lost everything in the 1958 coup d'état, and then rebuilt his fortune with his middle finger pointed at all those who had betrayed him. By the time we first met, Jacques had slowed down a bit – by then, he had forgotten more than I would ever know – yet he still possessed that mischievous spark and innate wisdom. I valued his counsel and mentorship almost as much as our friendship. Time and again he warned me that impostors and masqueraders could hurt us more than thieves and thugs, because they knew how to work our own weaknesses and aspirations to their advantage, and that I should be extra careful when I smelled that overly sweet, almost rancid stench of flattery in the air. Better a bad person than a fake one, as Jacques used to say.

Had I truly internalized the Big Sandy experience and Jacques's admonitions, the meeting with Melvin Collodi would never have happened. My alarm sensors should have gone off when Jim Morsel proposed a drink at the Four Seasons Hotel in Washington DC – one of the favourite watering holes of the city's rich and powerful, zand the wannabe rich and powerful. Jim and I had just wrapped up another useless meeting in a law firm on Capitol Hill discussing a mobile telephony licensing deal in Africa, and I had sworn to myself that I would never again waste my time with Jim and his wild fantasies. But Jim was a nice guy, and since he was self-aware enough to be adequately depressed about the meeting that had just ended, it seemed too cold-hearted to let him go drink by himself.

The Four Seasons bar is quite the scene, at the grotesque inter-section of gravitas and saccharine. Everyone there is just so important, and upon entering almost every guest scopes out the place in that very peculiar Washington method: a panoramic survey that glances over all the tables and chairs, eyes just slightly above the hairline of the closest person. Some call it the 'DC scalp look'. At its core, it is a search for the most promising opportunity to ingratiate oneself with someone of even greater importance. Even in his seriously deflated state, Jim did not omit the scalp look. Judging by his heavy sigh, the pickings were rather slim that evening, but just when I thought I would be able to escape after one quick drink, Jim said: 'Come, there's someone I'd like you to meet.'

We walked over to a corner table, where two men were sitting. Both seemed to be in their mid-fifties. One, very preppy looking, slim and fit, with perfectly coiffed hair, was dressed conservatively in a blue button-down shirt and striped tie. The other man was a little heavy, with pasty, almost ashen skin, sweating and obsessively devouring peanuts by the handful. Both were sporting the American flag lapel pin on their suit jackets.

'Daniel, I would like to introduce you to these two gentlemen,' Jim said, suddenly perking up. Directing his right hand, palm-side up, at the pin-up model of any self-respecting young Republican, he placed his left hand on my shoulders and announced: 'Meet Gerald Llewellyn. Gerald is the president of a very important think tank here in Washington.' And without giving me a chance to tell Mr Llewellyn how pleased I was to meet him, Jim turned to the other gentleman and pronounced, with all the gravitas he could muster: 'And this is Dr Melvin Collodi. I believe it is safe to say that Dr Collodi is one of the pre-eminent global experts on foreign policy and world affairs. He advises several Congressmen on the Hill. A real decision-former. An intellectual giant.' Before I had a chance to digest the importance of Gerald Llewellyn's think tank and the brilliance of Dr Melvin Collodi's mind with all the esteem they undoubtedly deserved, Jim proceeded to introduce me: 'Guys, this is Daniel Levin, the person I had mentioned to you. Daniel advises world leaders on economic development and political reform.'

I was stunned. Not so much because of the ridiculous hyperbole in the way he described me – after all, everything in Washington is so comically inflated that words lose all meaning and need to be discounted back to zero – but because of that sinking feeling that this meeting was not as spontaneous as I had originally thought. Evidently, Jim had discussed me with these two gentlemen, and from their body language it was evident that they had been expecting me. I was as annoyed at Jim for planning this ambush as I was at myself for so cluelessly falling for it, and resolved to excuse myself as soon as I could for some dinner appointment that must have completely slipped my mind.

Perhaps Dr Collodi was able to read my thoughts, because, just as I was plotting my escape, he said something that piqued my curiosity.

'It's a great pleasure and an even greater honour to meet you, Daniel,' he said in a charming, baritone voice, bordering on bass, with a slight Eastern European accent. 'I hope you don't mind if I call you Daniel. Please treat it as a sign of respect and veneration, and please do call me Melvin.'

That alone should have made me run for the doors. Respect – okay. But veneration? Really? It was so over the top, even by DC standards, that I almost burst out laughing. But then he added: 'I am a great admirer of your father. I consider him to be one of the greatest diplomats of the post-war era, and I often tell my students about your father's relationships with Archbishop Makarios and President Kenyatta as well as the other African leaders. For me, it has always been the perfect illustration of silent, relationship-based diplomacy. Didn't Kenyatta even name your sister?'

I was not expecting that. It was a little creepy. I'm all for doing one's homework and coming prepared, but this was stalker material. Not many people in my professional life knew about my father's diplomatic career and his efforts in Cyprus and Africa in the 1960s, and even fewer knew that Kenyatta had proposed the name 'Malaika' for my sister.

'You're right,' I replied. 'I'm impressed. The pleasure is all mine. But do tell me, how do you know about my father and Makarios and Kenyatta?'

'Well, Daniel, we were introduced many, many years ago in Vienna by a mutual friend. Your father was well known to aspiring diplomats such as myself, a deeply respected figure in our circles. And, if you will forgive me this uncouth instance of self-promotion: the Good Lord has blessed me with an extraordinary memory, and I never forget things that matter to me, including the smallest of details that others might not even pick up on.'

As it turned out, this was the one and only thing Melvin Collodi did not lie about: he did in fact possess a phenomenal memory.

Over drinks, Melvin and Gerald told me about their think tank. It sounded like a right-wing hack club – libertarians for dummies. The usual menu: less government, lower taxes, more freedom, nobody should have the right to take away our guns, don't mess with God, definitely don't mess with the Constitution, and all the good stuff. Gerald was very bland and sounded robotic while reciting their think tank's tenets and purpose, but he seemed like a nice enough guy. Even though Gerald was the president and Melvin just a policy adviser, it was apparent that Melvin, intense and idiosyncratic, was the alpha male in that relationship. Clearly highly intelligent and educated, he needed neither prompting nor context to regale his audience with his immense knowledge, and for no apparent reason I found myself on the receiving end of a short primer on twentieth-century European history, from the Bolshevik revolution to the wimpy Weimar Republic and the inevitable Third Reich, to the Soviet Union and communism – evil incarnate in Melvin's world order.

'Trust me, Daniel, I have suffered under the communists. They took everything from me, my wealth, my social standing, my freedom. But they could not take my dignity. They could not break me. America is the land built on freedom, it was my redemption, my salvation, and we should never take that for granted, Daniel. Never!'

Melvin had worked himself into a rage, his ashen-pinkish complexion now a deep red. He was sweating profusely, straight into the peanut bowl. It was impossible not to dislike this man, starting with his irritating habit of stating my name at the start of every sentence.

His rage evaporated just as fast as it had appeared, and within seconds he smiled. 'But enough about that, Daniel. *Tempi passati.* Let's talk about all the great things we can do together.'

'What is it you have in mind?'

I could tell that Jim was itching to say something, so I turned to him: 'Jim? Any thoughts?'

Jim was visibly nervous. He must have sensed that I was annoyed at having been set up with these two caricatures, so he coughed up a little sweet talk of his own for good measure, telling me that my name had come up in a previous meeting with Melvin and Gerald when they mentioned a speech I had recently given at a conference in London, and how surprised they were when he mentioned that he knew me.

At this point Melvin took over the conversation. 'Daniel, you cannot imagine how astounded Gerald and I were, and how delighted when Jim offered to introduce us to you. We have so much to discuss. So much in common.'

I highly doubted that. But by now my curiosity was aroused. 'What is it that you and Gerald would like to discuss with me?'

'Dubai, Daniel. Wonderful things are in store for us in Dubai. Greatness awaits us.'

'Please forgive me, but I am completely lost. What are you talking about?'

'Well, Daniel, where to begin? Let's start with Sheikh Mohammed. Or Sheikh Mo, as I call him.'

Melvin asked Jim to order another round of drinks, making two things rather clear: first, Jim would be paying for those drinks, and second, none of us would be going anywhere for a while. As Jim was chatting with the waitress, Melvin turned to Gerald with dramatic flair and asked: 'How far back do you think I should go to educate Daniel?'

Despite his clownish pomposity, which made his already unattractive features even more repellant, Dr Melvin Collodi radiated a certain charisma and intensity that was perversely captivating. I decided to give it a few more minutes, and one more drink.

'I suggest you fill in Daniel all the way from the beginning,' Gerald said. 'Very few people know Sheikh Mohammed as intimately as you do, and I'm sure Daniel will be fascinated by what you're about tell him.'

Gerald had clearly figured out the nuclear power of flattery, and Melvin smiled in childlike bliss. He sat back, loosened his tie and his belt buckle – a strange habit I would come to loathe. 'I haven't eaten all day,' he said, looking at Jim. 'Any chance you could get me something to eat? Something small, maybe a bagel with cream cheese?'

I could tell that Jim was annoyed by his demotion to culinary arranger, but he waved back the waitress and ordered Melvin's life-saving snack. 'The floor is all yours, Melvin, just the way you like it,' he said with a sardonic smile.

Was it ever! Melvin moved his face just inches away from mine – yet another horribly irritating habit – close enough for me to smell his breath and everything he had eaten that day.

'Daniel, please pay close attention. Everything I am about to tell you is the truth, the whole truth, and nothing but the truth. You must consider every word to be not only very important, but also highly sensitive. You have the reputation of being a trustworthy person, and your illustrious lineage allows me to share all this with you without demanding that you hold everything, every word I tell you in the strictest of strict confidence.'

Melvin looked straight into my eyes to ensure that I appreciated the depth and importance of the wisdom he was about to impart. He only averted his gaze when I nodded faintly.

'Very well, Daniel. Let me tell you about His Highness Sheikh Mohammed bin Rashid Al Maktoum, the ruler of Dubai and Prime Minister of the United Arab Emirates. Sheikh Mohammed, or Sheikh Mo for those like me who know him well, is one of the most impressive leaders I have ever met, and believe me, the list of leaders I have met is very long.'

'Tell him how you met Sheikh Mo,' Gerald interjected excitedly.

'Oh, it was the usual, the same way I am usually asked – no, begged! – to get involved. I got a call from his chief of staff, who told me that His Highness had read an article of mine on the putrefaction and inevitable fall of communism, and that he would very much like to meet me. I was a little busy at the time with several lectures and a manuscript I was working on, but I agreed to fly to Dubai. Of course, it was all taken care of by Sheikh Mo – first class on Emirates Airlines, VIP service upon arrival, and the suite at the famous Burj Al Arab hotel. You know, the one that looks like a giant sailboat.'

'He should have sent his personal 747 to pick you up,' I said. 'It's the least he could do!'

No reaction. Sarcasm was wasted on this man. He continued without missing a beat.

'Daniel, it was clear from the outset that Sheikh Mo was trying his damn hardest to impress me. On my first evening, he invited me to his private Majlis, where he receives his most honoured guests, and asked me to sit to his right – a gesture of utmost respect.'

The bagel and cream cheese arrived, and Melvin wasted no time in devouring the food. Strangely, he ate them separately. First the bagel, and then the cream cheese, licking it straight off the knife. There was something obsessive and frantic about his eating habits, and something extraordinarily nauseating. He then started to bite his fingernails and cuticles. Only later did I come to understand that he did this when he spun his stories to a spectacular degree, which explained why he had practically no fingernails and cuticles left.

'Where were we, Daniel? Oh yes, Sheikh Mo's Majlis. He made a point of telling me that there was a high-ranking delegation from Russia that had come to see him, but that he would keep them waiting, so overjoyed was he at my presence. Even though, frankly, I am hardly unaccustomed to being on the receiving end of such adulation, I can tell you that his effusiveness was, frankly, a little surprising, yet heart-warming.'

There it was, that word I so despised: frankly. That little self-awarded price, so prevalent in Washington, for speaking the truth. It was even more irritating than the equally ubiquitous 'to tell you the truth', perhaps because of the added serving of self-importance in the way it was usually enunciated. As a rule of thumb, its relation to the truth was coincidental at best, and often inversely proportional.

After a sip of his drink and a few more fingernail nibbles, Melvin continued: 'As nice as that first evening was, it was the next day, or rather the next night that took the cake. I had just settled in the couch at my hotel suite for some soothing Nietzsche reading, when my phone rang. Not my cell phone, but the hotel phone in my room. It was one of Sheikh Mo's guys, his personal assistant Abu Zayed. After apologizing profusely for inconveniencing me, he informed me that His Highness Sheikh Mohammed had instructed him to pick me up and bring me to His Highness. Despite the late hour and the unscheduled request, I was gracious about the whole thing and accepted the invitation. And thus begun a most memorable night.'

Jim had clearly heard this story more than once before. 'Tell Daniel what Sheikh Mohammed told you on your walk,' he interrupted Melvin. In other words, cut to the chase. But Melvin ignored him.

My eyes were starting to glaze over, and I desperately wanted to excuse myself for a bathroom break, but Melvin did not give me a chance to get a word in edgeways.

'Daniel, this was an unforgettable experience,' he continued. 'Abu Zayed treated me like a dignitary of the highest order, never forgetting to address me by my full title, opening and closing the car door for me, and apologizing repeatedly for disturbing me at such a late hour. He told me that his instructions were to take me to a special place, the spot where His Highness, may he continue to be blessed by the Almighty One, went to be alone with his thoughts. It was in the desert, lit only by the moon and the stars. We drove for about one hour, the last twenty minutes on sand. To be honest, Daniel, I was not sure what to make of this. Frankly, the thought did occur to me that Abu Zayed might be the most well-mannered kidnapper in history, and that I would never see my wife again. But I concluded that after all Sheikh Mo had not flown me all the way from the US to Dubai just to exchange a few pleasantries at his Majlis, seated on his right, the place of honour. I did mention that, right?'

'You did.'

'Well, Daniel, when we arrived he was waiting for us. All by himself, no staff, no security, no driver. He stood there, his white kandura and keffiyeh waving in the breeze. It was a sight to behold. Sheikh Mo looked like a mythical figure. If Mozart could have seen this, he would have changed his *Reine de la Nuit* to a *Roi de la Nuit*. Hahaha! What a tremendous wit I am! Do you get it? The king of the night instead of the queen of the night! Too funny!'

Jim looked at me with a bewildered look.

'Anyway, where was I?' Melvin continued. 'Oh yes, the desert. I got out of the car and greeted Sheikh Mo with appropriate respect. I was too entranced to notice that Abu Zayed had driven off without a word. "None of that tonight, Dr Collodi," Sheikh Mo said. "Tonight we will talk openly, man to man, brother to brother. No titles. Just you and me." Imagine, Daniel, how very extraordinary. This powerful man, a king in his kingdom, reaching out to me so intimately. Hard to imagine that my intellect alone could have impressed him so much.'

'Hard, but not impossible.' The words shot out of Jim's mouth before he could stop them.

Melvin's retort was swift and patronizing: 'Do us a favour, Jim. Be so kind and order us some more drinks.'

'Another round of cream cheese, too?' Jim was getting testy.

'No, Jim, just drinks. Thank you.' And with that Melvin turned back to me.

'Daniel, we walked for a good hour in complete silence. The cadence of our steps was in total synch. I am not a religious person, Daniel – the communists beat religion out of me! – but this was a very spiritual experience, very uplifting, very empowering. For some reason, I felt like I was swimming in the sea, like I was swimming through the Arabian Sea.'

'I'm surprised you were not *walking* across the sea,' Jim said. Clearly, he had reached his tolerance limit for Melvin's considerable pathos.

Gerald jumped in: 'Come on, Jim, take it easy. It's important for Daniel to get a full sense of how mind-boggling Melvin's experience with Sheikh Mohammed was.'

'You're right,' Jim backtracked. 'Sorry.'

Melvin continued without acknowledging Jim. 'Well, Daniel, after walking for more than one hour in complete silence, Sheikh Mo grabbed my arm and said: "Let's sit down. I would like to talk to you about something important. Nobody else knows about this, which is why I wanted to see you alone, without anyone else present." We sat in the sand, with our legs crossed, and I waited patiently for him to continue. And continue he did. "Every Monday evening, I come out here to be alone, my dear and trusted friend, my brother. I clear my mind and can think with my heart. I connect with the elements and with nature, and with the animals that inhabit it. There are moments – and this may sound strange to you – when this stage of meditation allows me to understand some of the animals. As you know, my brother, animals, and not just horses and falcons, are a big part of our Bedouin heritage. In fact, when I am at a certain place in Africa, there is a lion I can communicate with. But I digress. This is not the reason I brought you out here." And then he paused.'

Melvin finished his drink and handed Jim his empty cup with a gesture that demanded a refill. He turned back to me and continued.

'At this stage, Daniel, I was a little confused. I had no idea what to expect. Did he want me to advise him on the UAE's relationship with Washington? On containing Iran? Or did he want to get my take on how to handle his rich cousins in Abu Dhabi, the ones he would need to bail him out if the Dubai bubble ever burst? Perhaps he wanted me to take over the geopolitical education of his young son Hamdan, whom he had designated as Crown Prince? Or maybe I was completely off, and he wanted me to guide him on how to increase his chances of winning the Kentucky Derby – you know, the one trophy that has so painfully eluded him. After all, I do know a thing or two about race horses.'

I tried hard not to laugh out loud, especially since my bladder was about to explode. Jim was off ordering some more drinks, so I looked at Gerald to see whether I would find a little twinkle in his eyes, some acknowledgement that Melvin was laying it on a little too thick. But Gerald was completely fixated on Melvin. He seemed mesmerized by every word coming out of Melvin's mouth.

Once again, Melvin seemed to read my thoughts: 'I know, Daniel, I might sound immodest. But world leaders do ask me for advice and help in those matters, so it was only natural that I expected the leader of Dubai to do the same. Anyhow, Sheikh Mo had something else in mind. Something that leads back to you, Daniel.'

It would be a lie to say that Melvin did not have my full attention. All it took to rope me in was to give me a role in his story.

'Frankly, Daniel, what Sheikh Mo asked me for is simply tailor-made for you. Sheikh Mo wanted to know whether I knew of a way to help Dubai and the UAE develop financially out of their own internal human resources. He is seeking a catalyst for financial literacy and financial inclusion, and wants to generate political participation and a stakeholder mentality among his people. What he wants is a monarchy and a citizen state at the same time. To legitimize his monarchy by democratic means, beyond a mere popularity contest. And he wants to get there by developing his own, Emirati capacity, by investing in the next generation of leaders in his young country, not by flying in experts recommended by the World

Bank, or the IMF, or the McKinseys of the world. He wants a knowledge platform, which would also be able to transfer the necessary tools to these young leaders of the future. This is how he put it to me: "My brother, we might experience some growing pains and make a few mistakes along the path of our development, but this way at least these will be our *own* mistakes, not other people's mistakes imported by some outside experts who cannot possibly appreciate our cultural, political, and religious heritage." He told me that it was not only a matter of national pride and identity, but also of political survival and independence. And then he asked me whether I could help. Naturally, I immediately thought of you, Daniel.'

I was speechless. It was as if Sheikh Mohammed had drafted and delivered our firm's very own marketing pitch, just like Richard Muture's seductive tale that had lured me to Big Sandy, Texas. Every word he told Melvin could have been written by us, albeit not as concisely and persuasively. Sheikh Mohammed's vision and request to Melvin was a beautiful reflection of our firm's approach to development – from the need to rethink the Bretton Woods approach with the deeply flawed programmes of the World Bank and the IMF, to our own knowledge platform containing all the educational and infrastructure modules needed for effective development. I felt as though we had just won the lottery. Finally, a political leader who got it, who understood the need to empower the next generation of leaders, because the philosopher king that he was could not live forever. I ignored that tiny voice in my head, which was whispering that perhaps, just perhaps, this was all a little too perfect, too good to be true.

And just like that, I was caught in the net.

Melvin took another bite off the sad remnants of his fingernails. 'To tell you the truth, Daniel, I was very excited to find out that there were just three degrees of separation between us. And here's the wonderful part: I told Sheikh Mo about you, and his eyes lit up. He put his hand again on my arm and asked me to bring you to him. So there you have it. What do you think? Will you fly to Dubai with me?'

I should have reminded myself of the wonderful words that Jean de La Fontaine's fox speaks to the crow: *apprenez que tout flatteur vit aux dépens de celui qui l'écoute* – know that every flatterer lives at the expense of the one listening to him. But I didn't. Instead, I paid for the drinks, much to Jim's apparent relief, and told Melvin that I looked forward to Dubai, and that I would be in touch with some possible dates.

Jim walked me out of the Four Seasons. 'You and Melvin really seemed to hit it off,' he said, as we waited for my taxi. 'If you manage to impress Sheikh Mohammed as much as you impressed Melvin, great things could be in store for us.'

I returned to New York late that evening. I could not concentrate on anything other than the conversation with Melvin Collodi, and fantasies of exquisite initiatives with Sheikh Mohammed were swirling in my head. By the time I arrived home, my own excitement and imagination had worn me out.

When I walked into the office the next morning, our receptionist handed me two phone messages from Jim Morsel, with requests to call him back urgently.

Jim was clearly ready to go: 'Daniel, where have you been? Melvin has been calling me since six thirty this morning. He needs to talk to you urgently. He already spoke to Sheikh Mohammed and told him all about yesterday's meeting in the Four Seasons. It seems that Sheikh Mohammed is extremely excited to meet you. He absolutely loves everything about your background and your development platform. To quote Melvin, Sheikh Mohammed doesn't just want you, he wants you badly. If things pan out, you could become his principal adviser, the man he trusts.'

This would have been a good moment to take a short time out, to get some fresh air and a reality check. Instead, I was getting caught up in Jim's exhilaration.

Jim explained that I would fly to Dubai with Melvin, and that we had an appointment with Sheikh Mohammed the following Tuesday afternoon. He told me to expect a call later in the day from Melvin, who would undoubtedly fill me in on all the details.

I hung up and walked over to Gregg to fill him in. I had not yet had a chance to share any of these new developments with him. But I didn't even make it to his office.

'I have a Dr Melvin Collodi on the line for you, Daniel,' our receptionist shouted down the hallway. 'He says it's rather urgent. The gentleman sounded a little . . . different. Strange accent, too.'

I walked back to my office, closed the door, and picked up the phone.

Melvin got straight to the point: 'Well, Daniel, I had a long call early this morning with Sheikh Mo. I told him about our conversation in the Four Seasons yesterday, and that you were willing to fly to Dubai. Sheikh Mo was affirmatively ecstatic. He cannot wait to meet you. He has great plans for you. If I may say so, I do think I managed to set the table quite nicely for you, Daniel. I opened the door – you just have to walk through it. No need to thank me now, though even Sheikh Mo remarked how lucky you were to have me as a friend.'

I remained quiet, so Melvin continued: 'I have asked a friend of mine to take care of us in Dubai. His name is Adnan. He used to be with the police, and he knows everyone in Dubai. He happens to be on excellent terms with one of Sheikh Mo's best friends, an Emirati poet called Sultan, so it can't hurt for you to get to know Adnan. He's a nice enough guy. In any event, he will be very useful. Adnan desperately wants to impress me and be close to me. He will drive us around in that black Mercedes he is so proud of.'

'I am looking forward to meeting Adnan,' I responded. It was all I could think of to keep this conversation from becoming yet another Melvin monologue. His pompous, inflated style was unbearable, but my excitement at the prospect of this Dubai adventure made it all too easy to suppress my doubts and growing distaste for Melvin.

On Friday afternoon Jim called me to wish me good luck. 'Enjoy your thirteen-hour flight with Melvin' was his slightly facetious goodbye.

I had just arrived at JFK on Sunday evening and was about to check in, when my phone rang. It was Melvin, who sounded rather agitated.

'Well, Daniel, there is a slight problem. I am driving to New York from DC, and I am stuck in the most horrific traffic on the Turnpike. I don't think I will make the flight.'

I had that sinking feeling. Why was he driving from DC to New York, and why had he cut it so close? Something didn't feel quite right.

'Very sorry to hear that, Melvin. Should I cancel my flight, or move it to tomorrow?'

'Absolutely not, Daniel! Everyone is expecting you in Dubai, and I have asked Adnan to take excellent care of you. He will give you the Rolls-Royce treatment. I will take tomorrow afternoon's flight, and will be there on Tuesday morning, with plenty of time for our big meeting.'

I was not entirely unhappy to fly by myself, without the prospect of being regaled by Melvin's interminable stream of wisdom.

'Very well, then, see you on Tuesday morning,' I said and hung up.

I arrived in Dubai on a very steamy Monday evening. Adnan stopped by the hotel with two friends, and we hit it off instantly. Adnan was calm and soft-spoken, the total opposite of Melvin. We had a delicious dinner, engaged in pleasant and relaxed conversations. He told me that he would collect Melvin and me the next day in time for lunch. 'Assuming Melvin actually arrives in the morning,' he added with a mischievous wink.

I struggled to fall asleep that night. Only after Adnan had left did I realize that he never mentioned the appointment with Sheikh Mohammed. Of course, it was possible that Melvin had not clued him in, or that he had done so but sworn him to secrecy. But it was getting harder to dispel the doubts that were growing louder and louder, and I was starting to wonder whether flying to Dubai had been a mistake. The jetlag didn't help, either. I finally dozed off around five o'clock.

At eight a.m. the phone rang. It took me a moment to figure out where I was, and then, why I was there.

I answered with a hoarse voice. I must have sounded like I had a wicked hangover.

'Good morning, Daniel. Melvin Collodi here. Literally: here, hahaha. Rise and shine, my friend. I just arrived in the hotel. Of course, those idiots didn't have my room ready, but as soon as they realized who I was, they gave me a complimentary upgrade to a suite. I will shower and have a modest breakfast. Let's meet in the lobby in one hour.'

Melvin hung up without giving me a chance to reply or to ask him about our schedule for the day.

One hour later he was already waiting for me in the lobby, dressed in a three-piece suit – a rather questionable choice in Dubai's extreme heat and humidity – and reeking of aftershave.

'You're looking very dapper, Daniel,' he greeted me, clearly projecting.

'Thank you, you don't look too shabby yourself. I am relieved to see you. What are our plans for the day?'

'Well, Daniel, Adnan will pick us up in a few minutes and take us to meet Sultan.'

'Who?'

'Sultan, the local poet I told you about. Sultan is very close to Sheikh Mo, perhaps his closest friend. It will be very helpful for you to meet Sultan and to explain your platform to him. The more you impress Sultan, the more glowing the terms with which Sultan will describe you to Sheikh Mo. After our meeting with Sultan, Adnan will take us for a nice lunch.'

'When will we meet Sheikh Mohammed? I thought our appointment was for this afternoon.'

'Remember, Daniel, we are in the Persian Gulf. Actually, you should get in the habit of calling it the Arabian Gulf here. In any event, we will wait for the call to head over to Sheikh Mo's palace. This is the way it works here. There is no specific time, so we must just remain on standby. In the Arab world, standby can mean five

34

minutes, or it can mean a lifetime. Always look your best and be ready to dazzle Sheikh Mo whenever the bell rings, so to speak.'

Adnan arrived a few minutes later. Melvin made a huge spectacle of asking me to sit in the front of the car next to Adnan, opening the door with a theatrical swing of his arms. 'To the guest of honour, all the glory, and all the comfort,' he exclaimed, loud enough for everyone at the hotel entrance to hear. I caught Adnan rolling his eyes.

We arrived in Sultan's office twenty minutes later. Sultan welcomed us very graciously. He was mild-mannered and pleasant, and made me feel comfortable right away. We talked for almost two hours, covering US politics as well as the many conflicts in the Middle East and the Gulf. 'You don't light a match in the petrol station of the world,' Sultan said repeatedly, expressing his exasperation at all the sabre-rattling in the region. He was interested in our platform and its adaptability to a range of political and social cultures. It was evident that Adnan and Sultan were very close. And it was just as evident that Sultan did not care much for Melvin. He barely greeted him, and Melvin was uncharacteristically quiet during our time with Sultan. When we parted, Sultan held my hand as he walked us to the elevator, while Adnan and Melvin were a few steps behind us.

'I enjoyed talking to you,' he said. 'If you don't mind, I will ask Adnan to arrange for another meeting next time you are in Dubai by yourself.'

I was happy and flattered by Sultan's words, but at the same time also confused by the strange qualifier 'by yourself' at the end of his sentence. Was he trying to exclude Melvin? I shrugged off my doubts, and attributed these words to his awkward English.

'I'm glad I could introduce you to Sultan, Daniel,' Melvin said as we walked back to the car. He was back to his boisterous, pompous self, and wasted no time taking all the credit for the meeting with Sultan. 'He seemed to take a liking to you, which can only help when you meet Sheikh Mo. Sure, my recommendation carries some weight. Actually, considerable weight. But in Dubai, it cannot hurt to have a prominent local speak highly of you, too.'

During our drive to the restaurant, I was thinking about the conversation we had just had with Sultan. Something didn't add up. If Sheikh Mohammed was so infatuated with Melvin, and if Sultan was a close friend of Sheikh Mohammed, then why had Sultan just treated Melvin with such demonstrative contempt? Could it be that Sultan didn't know about Melvin's interactions with Sheikh Mohammed? Or was it possible that Sultan was jealous of the bond between Sheikh Mohammed – his close friend – and Melvin? I was thoroughly confused.

At lunch Melvin treated Adnan and me to an extensive lecture on geopolitics. His pearls of wisdom were laced with ugly stereotypes – the Americans were naive, the French were surrender-monkeys, the British present-day degenerates living in past glory, the Russians just a bunch of commu-fascists lusting to restore Greater Russia, the Chinese lacking in morality and caring only about their commercial interests, Indians corrupt to the core, and all Africans just totally hopeless.

'All of them?' I asked.

'Yes, Daniel, all of them, the entire continent, all one billion of them. They were better off in colonial days.'

Melvin was spewing some vile stuff, his saliva flying everywhere. But he reserved the crown jewel for the end.

'Listen to me, Daniel. If you will remember one thing, and one thing only from all the things I have taught you, then remember this: above all, don't trust the Arabs. Don't believe a word they tell you, not a word. There is no honour in their words. They are all liars.'

I was flabbergasted. 'If that is how you feel, Melvin, then what are we doing here?'

For a moment Melvin seemed stunned, at a loss for words to reply to what seemed to be a rather obvious and logical question. But he recovered quickly.

'Of course that is a generalization, Daniel. Someone as intelligent as you should know better than to take such general observations literally. I am trying to caution you to be careful when people here talk to you. The nicer they are, the more careful you need to be. In any event, just stick to me, and you'll be fine.'

I realized that we had lost Adnan halfway through Melvin's rants. Adnan had stepped outside to make a call, either bored or annoyed, I couldn't tell. Melvin leaned closer to me.

'I didn't want to say this in front of Adnan, but be careful, Daniel. Adnan is a typical Arab, he is always looking for his advantage. I would not be surprised if he tried to contact you directly and circumvent me, even though he only knows you through me, and even though he works for me and owes everything he has to me. If he tries to do that, please let me know immediately.'

I was very uncomfortable. I liked Adnan. He was composed and intelligent, with a quiet sense of humour.

'In any event, Daniel, we are waiting for the call from the palace to go to Sheikh Mo. As I told you this morning, this call could come anytime now, so be ready. Sheikh Mo might call me directly, which is probably why his friend Sultan was so rude to me in his office. In fact, I am certain Sheikh Mo will call me directly, as he has in the past.'

So that was why Sultan had ignored Melvin when we met before lunch? It seemed a little odd and out of character for a man as pleasant and unpretentious as Sultan to be jealous of Melvin's intimacy with Sheikh Mohammed, but not beyond the realm of possibility.

Adnan returned. 'I need to go to a meeting this afternoon, so I will drop you both off at the hotel and catch up with you later.'

Strange. No word about a meeting with Sheikh Mohammed.

Adnan came by the hotel late afternoon, together with his friend Jamal, a local Emirati from a prominent and wealthy family. Apparently, Jamal was having some troubles with the US authorities, and asked Melvin for advice.

'Leave this to me, Jamal,' Melvin said. 'This is a piece of cake for me. I will handle it straight with the White House. Consider it done.'

A visibly relieved Jamal invited us for dinner, and the rest of the evening was spent listening to Melvin's dissection of the Gulf's geo-politics and his prognostications for the upcoming tectonic shifts in the region. After a few glasses of wine, he also predicted the demise of the Gulf monarchies in three to five years. The meeting with Sheikh Mohammed did not come up.

The next day, I didn't hear from Melvin until late afternoon. When I asked him about the meeting with Sheikh Mohammed, his tone turned irritated and snippy.

'Well, Daniel, this is not fun for me, either. After everything I have done for this guy, all the advice I have given him, the least he could do is commit to a certain time. This is just so terribly discourteous. But what can we expect from these people?'

'Actually,' I answered, 'if we don't have a confirmation by to-morrow, I'm going to fly back to New York. I have a huge amount of work in the office, and cannot afford to stay in Dubai for no good reason.'

Melvin's tone changed immediately: 'Please, Daniel, you need to give this time,' he pleaded. 'This meeting *will* happen. But things take time in this part of the world. The Arabs have a saying that "time is like a sword – if you don't cut it, it will cut you", or some-thing like that. Anyway, I am inviting some friends for dinner tonight, and it would give me great pleasure if you could join us.'

Funny, Melvin's observation about time. I remembered some-thing Adnan had said over lunch after the meeting with Sultan, when Melvin lamented how every meeting here seemed to start late, how time seemed to have a different meaning here. Adnan had smiled and said that in the Gulf a watch was just a piece of jewel-lery – telling the time was a completely irrelevant function.

I accepted Melvin's invitation, but also made up my mind to fly home if things didn't change dramatically. Well, things did change dramatically, though not exactly in the way I had expected.

When I arrived at the restaurant, Melvin was already in the swing of things. Decked out in a charcoal-grey suit with thick pinstripes, a white shirt, and a pink tie, he looked as though he was cast in a mix of *The Godfather* and *Wall Street*. He was lecturing his other guests, an American with his Mexican wife, on the solution to the Palestinian problem, and introduced me without missing a beat. Melvin was in rare form, and none of us could get a word in edgeways for most of the evening. At some point, the couple asked me what had brought me to Dubai. Before I could answer, Melvin jumped in.

'Daniel is here with me. I am taking him to see Sheikh Mo. You know, Sheikh Mohammed. Sheikh Mo to his friends. Anyway, Sheikh Mo needs to talk to us about some important matters. But you know how it is here. These people are just pathological liars. They tell you one thing, and mean the other. They ask you to come, and then they make you wait. I am sick and tired of being disrespected. Sick and tired, I tell you. And I will be sure to tell Sheikh Mo, too.'

Melvin had quickly worked himself into a mini-rage. His face was all red and puffy, and for a moment I thought he was about to suffer a stroke.

'It's okay, Melvin,' I tried to calm him down. 'I understand that Sheikh Mohammed has a lot of things on his plate, and many people want a piece of him. I'm sure it will work out. He is just busy.'

'Busy? Busy?! Busy?!!' Melvin practically shouted. 'I'll give you busy! Do you know what I had to leave behind to come here? Do you know how many people are asking to see me back in the States? Do you know who I am?!'

At this point, the other guests in the restaurant were staring at our table. The maître d' came over and enquired if everything was okay. Melvin slowly calmed down.

'I'm sorry,' he said, 'this is all just so aggravating. I mean, just a few weeks ago, as I told Daniel, I was walking with Sheikh Mo and his friend Sultan in the desert in the middle of the night. He asked me – no, he begged me, to bring Daniel here. And now this.'

I heard nothing after 'Sultan'. Did he really say that Sultan was there when he was in the desert with Sheikh Mohammed? It couldn't be. During our meeting in the Four Seasons in Washington, Melvin had emphasized repeatedly that he and Sheikh Mohammed had been alone that night. No Sultan. No other person. I must have mis-heard him.

'Excuse me, Melvin, but was Sultan with you that night?'

'Of course, Daniel,' Melvin shot back. 'What a silly question. Anyone who knows Sheikh Mo knows that he always keeps Sultan around him at all times, like a pet.'

I didn't hear much else of what Melvin said that evening. I had a pit in my stomach. Suddenly, it all seemed to be one gigantic lie. I excused myself and stepped out of the restaurant.

The only person I could think of who might be able to shed some light on the situation was Adnan. I still had his business card in my jacket, and decided to call him. I hung up after three rings. Ten seconds later, he called me back.

'Hello, someone called me from this number?'

'Yes, Adnan, it's me, Daniel, the person you met with Melvin Collodi. I'm terribly sorry to bother you.'

'Good evening, Daniel, you're not bothering me at all. How are you?'

'Well, not so well, actually. I know this is a strange, and perhaps inappropriate, request, but is there any way we could meet in private?'

Adnan paused for a moment. 'Sure, where are you?'

'I'm at the restaurant in our hotel, I'm happy to come to you.'

'I'm near the airport,' Adnan said. 'The traffic to you is terrible at this time. Can you take a taxi to the Crowne Plaza on Sheikh Zayed Road, and I'll meet you at the bottom of the ramp in front of the main entrance. We can then drive somewhere quiet.'

'Thank you, Adnan, I really appreciate it. One more thing: please don't mention this to Melvin. I will explain everything when we meet.'

I returned to our table, just as Melvin's guests were paying for dinner. It seemed that Melvin had not taken the 'invitation' part of his invitation all that literally. I excused myself, telling Melvin and his guests that I wasn't feeling well, which was the truth. I immediately found a taxi at the hotel entrance, and spent the duration of the ride revisiting all of Melvin's statements, wondering whether any of them had been true. If he had lied about Sultan being with Sheikh Mohammed in the desert, had the rest been a lie, too?

Twenty minutes later I arrived at the Crowne Plaza. Adnan was already there, and I got into his car.

During the drive, we talked about our families, and Adnan told me about his work and some of his friends. He told me that he and Sultan were very close, and that they had known each other for over twenty years. We stopped at a nice spot in Jumeirah, near the beach, and found a quiet table.

I was not sure how to begin, so I started with another apology: 'I am really sorry for dragging you out here. This is not something I would ordinarily do. I met you through Melvin, and I know that it seems inappropriate for me to bypass him and contact you directly.'

'Please don't apologize again, Daniel. It is my pleasure. Besides, I don't really like Melvin.'

'You don't?'

'No. Not at all. I can't stand the guy.'

I was thoroughly confused. 'I thought you and Melvin were close friends? That's what he told me back in the US. Why would you spend all this time with us, if you don't like Melvin?'

Adnan leaned back in his chair and was quiet for a few moments. He seemed to be pondering how to break some bad news to me. After a while, he turned to me with a faint smile.

'Last time Melvin came to Dubai, I swore to myself that I would never meet with this man again. He embarrassed me in front of Sultan. As you know, Sultan is not an insignificant person in Dubai. He is one of Sheikh Mohammed's closest friends, and for good reason. He is extremely intelligent, and very kind. He has a pure heart. But Melvin put me in a bad situation. During his last visit, he pestered me to meet Sheikh Mohammed, so I took him to Sultan in the hope that Sultan would agree to take him to the palace.'

Adnan paused, clearly pained by the memory of it all.

'So what happened?' I asked.

'It was a disaster. The moment he stepped into Sultan's office, Melvin started to lecture him on politics and on how the Arabs don't appreciate everything that America has done for them. I could tell that Sultan took an immediate, visceral dislike to Melvin. Sultan is normally a very gentle man, who never uses harsh words. But after a few minutes of Melvin's diatribes, Sultan turned to me and said in Arabic: "Get this rabid dog out of here before he dirties my carpet." I had never, ever heard Sultan speak that way. Never!'

I was in shock. Over the span of just a few moments, it had all come tumbling down. Melvin's house of lies had collapsed. Still, I had to ask.

'So Sultan never took Melvin to see Sheikh Mohammed?'

Adnan looked at me like I had five heads.

'Of course not. I ended that meeting with Sultan immediately. I spent the two following weeks apologizing to Sultan.'

'So why did you take us to Sultan yesterday?'

'Because I like you, Daniel. I enjoyed meeting you, and I was sure that Sultan would, too.'

I was flattered. 'Thank you, Adnan. That was very kind. It was a pleasure meeting Sultan, and I hope it wasn't too painful for him.'

'Not at all,' Adnan said. 'Sultan liked you very much, and when we left he told me that he would gladly take you to Sheikh Mohammed, so long as I never show up with Melvin again.'

I decided to ask one more time. 'So Sultan really never took Melvin to Sheikh Mohammed?'

'Never,' Adnan shot back, his tone now a little impatient.

'And Melvin never met Sheikh Mohammed without Sultan?'

'Come on, Daniel, what are you talking about? Do you really think that someone like Melvin could get anywhere near Sheikh Mohammed without Sultan? He never met Sheikh Mohammed, and he's been angry about it ever since that visit a few months ago. Every time he calls me, he goes off on that, how I promised to arrange for him to meet Sheikh Mohammed, and how we Arabs are all just a bunch of market storytellers.'

There it was. It had all been one big lie. I felt a rage brewing inside me.

'I can't believe Melvin made all this up. And I can't believe he, of all people, called all Arabs liars. Does this guy have no shame?'

Adnan smiled sardonically. 'Shame is an utterly wasted emotion for a man like Melvin.'

I was devastated. I felt like such a fool. The warning signs had all been there, in plain sight, but I had been too blinded by my own fantasies to pay attention to them.

'I don't understand,' I told Adnan. 'What could he possibly have hoped to achieve with all these lies? It makes no sense at all. Think about it, how could this possibly have played out in a good way for Melvin? Either we don't get to see Sheikh Mohammed, in which case Melvin looks like an idiot, or – even worse – we do by some miracle get to see Sheikh Mohammed because Sultan takes pity on us, and Melvin is unmasked as the pathological liar that he is when it becomes obvious that Sheikh Mohammed has never seen this man before. This is sheer madness!'

'You are right, Daniel,' Adnan said after a lengthy pause. 'It makes no sense. My only explanation is that he counted on the fact that Sultan would like you and agree to take you to Sheikh Mohammed, and because Melvin had been the one to bring you to Dubai, Sultan would reward him by taking him along, too. And once we would be sitting with Sheikh Mohammed, Melvin would not open his mouth, the same way he kept quiet when we visited Sultan a few days ago. And if Sheikh Mohammed happened to greet Melvin with a "pleased to meet you", Melvin would later tell us that in fact Sheikh Mohammed had misspoken, and that he really had intended to say "pleased to meet you *again*". Remember, Daniel, this guy might be a pathological liar, a psychopath, perhaps, but he is not stupid.'

'Maybe,' I said. 'Maybe that really was Melvin's grand plan. Or maybe he is a liar with a death wish.'

'What do you mean?' Adnan asked.

'Maybe subconsciously he wanted to get caught, to be put out of his miserable existence.'

Adnan laughed. 'You are giving him too much credit, Daniel. That would actually require a certain degree of integrity and introspection, which the great Dr Melvin Collodi clearly lacks. No, I think the answer is much, much simpler: he believes his own lies.'

Adnan was probably right. Melvin seemed to inhabit a different planet, where fiction and reality were one and the same. I felt totally deflated, exhausted by the whole experience.

I managed to avoid Melvin during the next thirty-six hours that I remained in Dubai. When it was time to leave, Adnan drove me to the airport, and we parted as friends.

There was one thing left for me to do. I had never asked my father about Melvin. I called him from the airport lounge.

'Hi Dad, it's Daniel.'

'Hi Daniel, how are you? Where are you?'

'I'm fine, Dad. I'm at the airport in Dubai, about to leave for New York.'

'Dubai? What are you doing there?'

'It's a long story, I'll tell you about it some other time. Just a quick question: do you know someone called Melvin Collodi?'

'Who? Can you repeat that name, please?'

'Melvin Collodi. He claims to have met you many years ago in Vienna.'

'Oh yes, I vaguely remember. He was with a business contact of mine, Paul or Peter something or other, I can't remember his family name. Why?'

'I was curious what you thought of this Collodi fellow.'

My father was quiet for a moment, then said: 'All I remember is that he was extremely unlikeable, very full of himself. He had a disgusting habit of eating his fingernails, and he kept dropping the names of important people. He seemed a little unhinged, and I got the impression that he was making this stuff up as he was talking. I didn't believe a word he was saying. Why do you ask?'

'Never mind, Dad. It's not important. Good night.'

Breakfast at the UN

Shortly after returning from Dubai, I met my friend Peter Haffert for lunch. Peter was a retired United Nations diplomat, and he and his wife Kisi were two of the nicest and most intelligent people I knew. Peter could tell from my subdued demeanour that something was troubling me. I told him about the Dubai adventure, how easily I had been seduced by an outlandish storyteller like Melvin Collodi, and how disappointed I was in my ability to read people. I had lost faith in my own judgement. Peter tried to cheer me up.

'These types of experiences will help prepare you for the courts of the really powerful,' he consoled me. 'Don't feel dejected, think positive. Kisi always tells me to be an optimist today, and leave regrets for later.'

I laughed. Peter's sunny disposition was balm for my soul.

'Anyway,' Peter continued, 'at least you have some excitement in your life. You get to meet real, colourful villains. Think about what I had to put up with all those years at the UN. Just the other evening I was invited to a reception at some ambassador's East Side residence, where a former colleague, a European ambassador, bragged about the three weeks he and his wife got to spend at a luxury resort in the South Pacific for a UN island conference. And this ambassador's country is landlocked, has never sniffed seawater! When I asked him why he had gone, since this conference was so obviously irrelevant to his country, he gave me this pitying look and walked away. He was not going to waste any more time with someone who lacked the requisite appreciation for the perks of the job. But even more than this rampant sense of entitlement, it was the unbearable boredom of it all that made me retire early.'

'Right now, I could handle a bit of boredom,' I countered.

'Sure, you say that now on the heels of this awful experience in Dubai,' Peter said, 'but remember all the nonsense that comes with the boredom. At the UN, the bullshit meter is off the charts. In fact, if we could impose a fee on all that bullshit, the UN's funding problems would be forever solved. But, as I said, let's think positive. Just like the UN can get it right once in a while, I am sure you will encounter some wonderful people on your journey. And speaking of wonderful people, I have invited a few friends for dinner to our home on Thursday evening. Why don't you join us?'

I gladly accepted Peter's dinner invitation. I always enjoyed the gatherings at his lovely home full of beautiful African artefacts, and the evening would be a welcome distraction.

The meal was delicious, and we spent the evening talking about Africa, the promise and the disappointment, and, above all, the shattered dreams. There always was a deep sadness in Peter's eyes when he lamented how it had all gone downhill, but he also expressed hope that future generations would have a greater sense of community and responsibility towards this abused and pillaged continent.

Over dinner Peter introduced me to Andrea, a friend of Kisi's and former colleague of his, who was heading a UN programme that focused on developing cities in this age of massive urbanization – Andrea called them 'sustainable human settlements'. Andrea was very bright and engaging, and soon we were immersed in an intense conversation about the need for massive property-rights reform. Andrea asked me to explain how I would go about fixing this problem in Africa. I made the case for an Africa-wide initiative to codify and simplify property rights, to get a critical mass of people to register their property for the first time, and to incorporate all tribal and religious norms in the local property-registry systems, even for some of the nomadic societies with their very specific challenges. I thought that a joint initiative with Andrea's UN team could have a seismic effect. Andrea listened intently. I was on a roll, encouraged by Andrea's concentrated demeanour.

About ten minutes into my pleading, Andrea deadpanned, 'It's never going to happen.'

I was taken aback. 'Why not?' I asked.

'Because nobody will register his property, if it means that he could be taxed on it. And nobody will agree to be taxed on a property, if the state does not provide basic services and infrastructure, such as clean water, roads, sewage, schools, hospitals. It's that simple. Forget about property rights.'

I couldn't think of an intelligent retort, so all I mustered was a meek 'Are you sure?'

'Very sure, Daniel,' Andrea shot back. 'Believe me, you are not the first blue-eyed idealist who thinks he can fix this problem in Africa. My friend Hernando de Soto thought he could do it, too. He thought that he could do in a place like Egypt the same thing that he had successfully done in his native Peru. He learned that he couldn't. This is Africa! This continent can humble anyone, no matter how great and accomplished.'

'That's a little deflating,' I said.

'Perhaps,' she said. 'But if you really want to put your enthusiasm and resources to good use, why don't you support my personal political campaign. My term at the UN is coming to an end, and I'm considering a run for parliament in my home country.'

I was dumbstruck. In one and the same breath Andrea had just killed a UN project that was precisely within the scope of her mandate, and moved seamlessly to soliciting support – UN-speak for cash – for her own post-UN career. Suddenly, flashes of Big Sandy and Dubai appeared before my eyes. Once again I had allowed my own myopic enthusiasm and aspirations to get the better of me, only to reveal my naiveté. I was at a loss for words, and Andrea must have recognized that I probably was not going to be useful to her. She looked at me with a smile that exuded both boredom and contempt, and said 'It was nice talking to you.' And with that, she stood up and left.

Ten minutes later I was still sitting by myself, licking my wounds, when Peter walked up to me with an older gentleman.

'Daniel, I would like to introduce you to another friend of mine, Andy Gelder. I am sure the two of you will hit it off.'

I had heard of Gelder. He was one of the most successful venture capitalists in New York and a major donor to the Democratic Party.

'Peter told me good things about you, Daniel, and the work that you do,' Gelder said. 'If you don't mind, I'd like to put you in touch with a close friend of mine, one of the top people at the United Nations Development Programme.'

'That's very kind of you, Andy, I appreciate that,' I replied a little distracted, still reeling from my encounter with Andrea. 'Forgive me, please, but I think I've had enough UN exposure for one evening, though it's nice of you to offer.'

'I understand,' Gelder said. 'The UNDP – actually, the UN as a whole – isn't my cup of tea, either. But these guys have been hitting me up for funding. They call it PPP, public-private partnership. They must think we're complete fools. I mean, I must have the word "idiot" tattooed on my forehead. Obviously, PPP is just a euphemism for trying to find private-sector suckers to pay for their meaningless, underfunded, brain-dead projects.'

'Forgive me, but if that's how you feel, why would you want me to contact this UNDP person?' I asked.

'Because he's been talking to me about financial literacy, and the need to develop from within, not through external advisers. This person seems to be relatively serious. And when Peter told me about you and your platform, it just made sense to put you in touch with this guy. I made it clear that I would only fund something that was real, that could be successful and sustainable, not their usual debate-club, never-ending conference-going nonsense. Just call him, and if it's too irritating, feel free to drop the matter. I'll have my secretary send you his contact details and also make sure that they are expecting your call at the UNDP, so you don't get the usual runaround.'

I received the information the next morning, but couldn't bring myself to call. I shared much of Peter's reservations about the UN, but very little of his optimism. There had just been too many disappointments, too much wasted time, too many meaningless meetings and communications.

A week after the dinner at Peter's home, I met him for lunch, and he asked me whether I had followed up with Gelder's contact at the UN. A little embarrassed – it felt ungrateful – I confessed that I had not. Peter encouraged me to get in touch with them. He assured me that Gelder's word carried great weight at the UN – 'he who pays the piper calls the tune' – and that this time it would be worth my while. I promised Peter that I would contact them.

Back in the office, I dialled the number that Gelder's assistant had given me.

'Mr Dellin's office, please hold,' a voice answered.

Thirty seconds later, the voice was back. 'Mr Dellin's office. What can I do for you?'

'Good afternoon, my name is Daniel Levin.' I did not make it past my name before the voice interrupted.

'Who?'

'Daniel Levin. I got your number from Andy Gelder.'

'Who?'

So much for Peter's assessment that the UNDP staff would turn into a pillar of salt at the mere mention of Gelder's name.

'Andy Gelder,' I said. 'Mr Gelder and Mr Dellin know each other well.' Again, I did not make it very far.

'Listen, David . . .'

'It's Daniel.'

'Listen, Daniel. We are extremely busy around here. We have the annual meetings coming up, and Mr Dellin is running from one important appointment to another. I'll be sure to let him know you called.'

'That would be most kind of you,' I said, in a tone that was more sarcastic than I had intended it to be. She hung up without a word.

Within ten seconds I had purged this exchange from my memory as yet another useless UN experience.

One week later, I got a call from Mr Dellin's assistant.

'This is Anita from Mr Dellin's office,' she said. If I tried really hard, I could detect a sliver of a slightly less unpleasant lilt in her tone.

'Hello, Antonia,' I answered, deciding to have some fun.

'It's Anita,' she shot back. The slight improvement in her tone had evaporated as rapidly as it had appeared.

'I'm so sorry, Anita, I'm terrible with names.' Which happens to be true.

'Anyhow, Daniel, I have been asked to contact you to set up a breakfast meeting with Mr Dellin and his team. The next two weeks are not convenient for Mr Dellin. How about three weeks from today at nine in the morning?'

On the day of the meeting I showed up in the main lobby ten minutes early, as instructed by Anita. After giving my name and having my picture taken, I was handed a visitor badge and asked to wait. Fifteen minutes later, a young lady showed up and asked me to follow her. I was fairly annoyed that I would be late for this meeting through no fault of my own, but my guide was so lovely that I decided to let it go. It turned out that she was a law student from Kenya, spending the summer in New York for an internship at the UN. Her name was Miriam, and when I asked her whether she had been named after Miriam Makeba, her face lit up.

'You know Miriam Makeba?' she asked with a big smile.

'I do. I lived in Kenya in my childhood. In fact, my sister was born there and was named after one of Miriam Makeba's songs – Malaika.'

'No way! When did you live there?' Miriam asked, still beaming.

'A long time ago, in the sixties.'

'The sixties?! You're old!' she laughed.

Miriam could have said anything to me – with that wonderful smile, it was charming.

We had reached our floor, and Miriam walked me to the conference room where the meeting was going to take place.

'Will you be joining us?' I asked.

'I'm afraid not. I'm just an intern,' Miriam replied, still with the same delightful smile. 'The people you will be meeting are all very, very important. Good luck.'

*

I entered a room full of people. After shaking many hands and being introduced to names I forgot almost as soon as they were uttered, I found myself holding a huge stack of business cards with the blue UN department logos. This for an intimate breakfast meeting that was supposed to be between Mr Dellin and myself. It seemed like half the United Nations staff was squeezed into the conference room: two gentlemen representing the Secretary General's office, two from the United Nations Democracy Fund, three from UNCTAD, two from UNESCO, one representing the World Food Programme, and a few others who did not identify themselves. But UNDP took the prize: they had fifteen people at the meeting. Fifteen! From the Regional Bureau for Africa, to the Partnerships Bureau, to the Foundations Affairs Partnerships Bureau, to – my personal favourite – the head of Donor Relations from the Division for Resources Mobilization – also known as the person looking for others to pay the UNDP's bills.

The one person who had not showed up was Mr Dellin himself. Apparently, some very important and sensitive matter had kept him from attending. At the UN all matters are very important and sensitive, as they should be when one is saving the world.

Lisa from the UNDP's Foundations Affairs Partnerships Bureau took the lead. 'Welcome, Daniel, to this morning's meeting. Is it okay if we stick to first names?'

'Of course,' I answered. 'It will be difficult enough for me to remember those.'

Lisa smiled. 'I know, we're quite a large group. Mr Dellin, who is very sorry he couldn't be here today, asked us to meet with you and to hear your thoughts on financial education, capacity building, and all that. Many of the people in this room have some personal or professional connection to Africa, so perhaps you could keep that in mind during our discussion.'

I was irritated that Dellin was not there, and that neither he nor his office had called me out of courtesy to reschedule. As tempting as it would have been to get up and leave, I couldn't do so without seeming arrogant and rude, which would have put me right up there – or, rather, down there – with Dellin. So instead, I spent the next ten minutes talking about our approach to financial literacy and capacity building, about the convergence of political and financial inclusion, and about the need to transfer the know-how and the necessary tools to a local group of leaders, preferably future leaders, the next generation, in order to maximize the returns of this investment in the future of a particular country.

When I finished, Lisa thanked me and invited her colleagues to join in the discussion. There were a few questions, some to the point and some way off the mark. Then Ken from the Africa Bureau raised his hand.

'Thank you, Daniel, for sharing your approach with us. Would you mind if I told you about our own methodology when it comes to financial literacy and capacity building?'

'Of course not,' I replied, relieved at not having to do any more of the talking.

'Well, we tackle this important challenge from a slightly different, quite possibly better angle, if you don't mind me saying so. For us, these issues cannot be separated from microfinance initiatives. They are intertwined, connected at the hip, if you will. In some way, they are one and the same.'

'Microfinance?' I asked. I had no idea why Ken would bring that up in *this* context. I knew that microfinance was the flavour of the moment at the UNDP and the World Bank, but how financial literacy and microfinance were the same thing was beyond me.

'Yes, Daniel, microfinance,' Ken answered. His tone was slightly patronizing. 'Allow me to explain it to you.'

For the next twenty minutes Ken proceeded to lecture me on the common denominator between microfinance and public education, not just in the financial domain, but throughout all educational challenges. Health education, vocational training, university education, religious education, everything. Even sex education. He was making no sense whatsoever. Microfinance had its value, of course, in providing banking and financial services to the many millions who lacked such access. But to exalt it as a panacea for all ills, even beyond economic woes, made little sense to me.

I could tell that his colleagues were starting to get antsy. A few times Lisa tried to interrupt him, but Ken would have none of that. He was on a roll, gearing up for the grand finale.

'So you see, Daniel, what I am trying to explain to you is that all you need to focus on is providing effective microfinance in a country, and all the rest will follow. There is no need for fancy knowledge platforms or the transfer of tools and skills. Take care of microfinance, and microfinance will take care of the rest. It's as simple as that.'

I didn't know what to say, and hoped someone else would jump in, but no such luck.

'Well, Daniel, what do you think?' Ken asked me, looking straight in my eyes.

'It's interesting,' I said, hoping to bring an end to the conversation.

'I *know* it's interesting,' Ken shot back. 'I don't need *you* to tell me that. What I would like to hear is what you think of our methodology.'

'I'm not sure I fully follow your thoughts,' I started carefully. 'If I understood you correctly, you are saying that good microfinance institutions will also solve all the educational shortcomings in a country. Is that right?'

'Exactly,' Ken proclaimed with a triumphant smile. 'I knew you would understand.'

'Well, I'm not so sure I understand. I don't really see the connection.'

Ken let out an exasperated sigh.

'It's really not that complicated. You have microfinance, you have money. You have money, you have education. How hard is that?'

The others in the room were clearly restless, and I concluded that escalating it with Ken would only prolong the agony of this meeting. I decided to play nice and end this misery on a pleasant note.

'Forgive me, Ken, I must be a little dense. Perhaps it would be easier for me to understand your approach if you gave me concrete examples of countries in which you have successfully tested and implemented your methodology. That would be helpful.'

Ken looked at me in surprise. 'This hasn't yet been implemented.'

My turn to be surprised. 'It hasn't?' I asked.

'Nope. This is an approach I have been working on together with an economist at the World Bank. We're getting close to a launch.'

Now I really didn't know what to say. All this blabber about some theory Ken and his World Bank buddy had been cooking up in their basement? I had wasted half an hour of my life listening to this guy. Half an hour I would never get back.

'Just out of curiosity, how long have you been working on this theory?' I asked.

'Oh, we've been at this for the past five years. We're getting close,' Ken replied.

Five years! All this time, using up resources, no testing, no verification, no reality check with people who actually worked in the field, who could have told Ken and his World Bank buddy that they were smoking something. Ken had displayed zero self-doubt during his brilliant oration. It was just too absurd. I had been exposed to a lot of silliness and ineffectiveness at the UN, but never before to anything like this.

'Did you not feel the need to test your theory? Stress-test it? See if it works, what impact it has, figure out which aspects require some adjustments in order to be effective and sustainable?' I asked.

'Don't be silly,' Ken replied without hesitation. 'Of course not. There's no need for all those tests. Our theory is rock-solid. Granite, if you will.'

'But what makes you so sure your theory will work in practice?' I asked, still not sure whether Ken was speaking tongue-in-cheek.

Ken did not miss a beat. 'Oh, I'm sure all right, Daniel. Contrary to what you cynics think, microfinance is the new gospel. It is what will take us in Africa to the Promised Land. Some things you just know, Daniel. You know them not just in your head, but also in your heart, in your gut. You don't need to test them. Microfinance is one of them. Our theory is axiomatic, it cannot fail.'

'But what makes you so sure?' I asked again, stunned by Ken's almost religious absolutism.

'Because this time we've gone above and beyond the call of duty. We not only believe our theory is correct, actually a categorical imperative, dare I say. No, this time we've even consulted a few microfinance experts, gathered some data,' Ken said beaming, ostensibly pleased with himself. 'You've just got to appreciate that.'

'My goodness, Ken, what do you want me to do, throw you a parade?' I shot back, faster than I should have.

'Excuse me?' Ken asked, genuinely confused.

'Seriously,' I said, a little more calmly. 'You are *supposed* to look at other projects, you are *supposed* to gather and evaluate data and evidence. You are *supposed* to test and verify your virgin theories, see whether they work, and figure why they don't or what improvements they require. You are expecting applause for doing what you are *supposed* to be doing, for just doing your job. Which, by the way, you clearly didn't.'

'Oh, people like you always think you're smarter than we are,' Ken said, visibly piqued. 'You come into our house, and then you criticize us. What makes you sure you're so brilliant?'

'I never said I was brilliant,' I replied, no longer able to hide my irritation. 'But at least I'm painfully aware of the fact that I am not brilliant. It's always the wrong people who end up questioning their own convictions.'

Ken seemed lost. 'I am sensing a lot of hostility,' he said, changing track. 'Why always so negative?'

I made one last attempt at a civil and rational conversation. 'I'm sorry if I seem negative. It's just that you could do so much with the infrastructure and the resources of the United Nations behind you. Instead, your approach seems uninformed and even reckless. There's nothing wrong in believing in the power of microfinance, if that's what floats your boat. But you still have an obligation to check whether your theory works. I'm aware of the fact that microfinance is a fashionable concept these days. Sometimes, I get the impression that there is one microfinance initiative per citizen in certain parts of Africa. But still, you cannot be sure that your theory works if you have not tested it, exposed it to challenges and criticism. Microfinance is not a religion, even if it feels that way occasionally. With all due respect, I have the impression that you are substituting knowledge with opinion, and the less you know, the stronger your opinions seem to be.'

Ken gave me this strange look, at first utter surprise, and then followed immediately by righteous indignation. 'Really? So if I come up with a theory, it is just an opinion. But if you come up with one, it's knowledge? Is that how it works?'

'No,' I said, desperately wishing to end this conversation. 'That is not how it works, and that is not what I said. What I was trying to express is that what you and your colleague lack in knowledge, you make up for in opinions. I'm not trying to insult you. Remember, you asked me what I thought of your approach. Perhaps we should just leave it at that and call it a day.'

Ken gave me this strange, confused look. Clearly, he had never even for a moment considered testing or verifying his theories. All you had to do is classify them as 'axiomatic', as he put it, and all questions of authority were settled. As simple as that.

'But what is it to you, Daniel? What do you care?' Ken asked.

We had just left Planet Reason. Time to end this.

'Seriously, Ken,' I said as calmly as I could. 'Can't you see that it is plain wrong to unload your untested theories on unsuspecting, innocent societies, just because the United Nations and the World Bank provide you with the authority and the opportunity to do so?'

Ken pondered for a moment, as if he was giving serious thought to my question. 'Not really. I don't see that,' he finally replied.

'Well then, it might be time to wrap this up,' I said. 'Thank you for your time.'

Only now did I realize that the entire room had gone silent. I was too exhausted to be bothered by the tension.

Lisa must have sensed my deflation. 'Thank you, Daniel, for meeting with us,' she jumped in, 'and, again, our apologies that Mr Dellin could not make it. Let's stay in touch.'

I stood up and muttered a group goodbye. I couldn't leave this conference room fast enough.

Outside the door, Miriam was waiting.

'You are a sight for sore eyes,' I said, smiling at her.

'How did it go?' she asked, as we waited for the elevator.

'It was an out-of-body experience,' I answered. 'The best part of this morning was meeting you.'

Miriam looked at me with her magnificent smile. 'What happened?' she asked.

'It's always the same story,' I said. 'I don't know why I keep allowing myself to be talked into coming here. Every time, I leave this building with a few new ulcers. It's so frustrating!'

'Hahaha,' Miriam laughed. 'I assume you've met Ken . . .!'

I nodded.

'On my very first day here,' Miriam continued, 'Ken asked me out to dinner. When I refused, he arranged for me to be assigned to him as my mentor. Fellow Kenyan to fellow Kenyan, so to speak. I spend most of my time here trying to avoid him.'

'My heartfelt condolences,' I said. 'He is one of the most incompetent people I've met here, and that's quite an accomplishment. I wish he was European, or South American, or Asian, or anything but African. People like Ken keep compounding the negative stereotypes about Africa. Why does it have to be that way?'

'Don't worry, Daniel,' Miriam said with a smile. 'I refuse to let Ken speak on my behalf or on behalf of my country, let alone my continent.'

'Fair enough.'

'Anyway, don't concern yourself with Ken,' Miriam said. 'Sometimes, the dumber people are, the smarter they think they are.'

Miriam was one of those rare individuals who could say the harshest thing with the most innocent, charming demeanour. A born assassin. I made myself a mental note to stay on Miriam's good side, should we ever meet again.

We had arrived at the ground floor.

'You asked why it has to be that way with Africa,' Miriam said as we left the elevator. 'If you have a moment before you leave, I would like to share with you a joke my father once told me.'

'Of course,' I said. 'I could use some cheering up.'

'I'm not sure it will cheer you up,' she said, 'but I'll give it a try. Well, as my Dad used to say, Africa is just *so* special! Consider this: at independence, some African countries had approximately the same GDP as a place like Singapore had at its independence. And look at the situation today! When you asked why it has to be that way, I immediately thought of that story my Dad told me about the African student and the Southeast Asian student studying at Oxford in the fifties, before their countries' independence. Do you know this joke?'

'I don't.'

'Well,' Miriam continued, 'the two became close friends. After their studies, they returned to their respective countries and got involved in politics. Since they had both studied economics, they were the obvious choices to serve as their countries' first finance ministers after independence. A few years later, the African fellow visited his Southeast Asian colleague – let's just say it was in Singapore to make this easier. He looked out of the office window and saw an amazing city-state rising. New buildings, new roads, new hospitals, new schools. He was deeply impressed. "How did you do this?" he asked his Singaporean friend. "Actually, it was quite easy," the Singaporean minister answered. "Let's say we needed a new road. I published the terms and conditions, we conducted a tender, some company got the bid, I kept ten per cent for myself, the work got done, and everyone was happy." His African colleague took it all in. "I'll keep this in mind. What you have accomplished here is just terrific." Well, a couple of years later, the Singaporean minister paid a return visit to his friend in Africa. Looking out of a window in the ministry of finance, all he saw were decrepit shacks, unpaved roads, open sewers. "What happened?" he asked in horror. "I thought we had talked about this. What went wrong?" "I have no idea," his African colleague answered. "I followed your example and did exactly as you told me. We needed a new road, so I published the terms and conditions, did a tender, some company won the bid. I kept one hundred per cent for myself, and nothing got done. It's a mystery to me!" Every time I am reminded of this joke, Daniel, I don't know whether I should laugh or cry.'

'Probably a little of both,' I said. 'I should have just had a coffee with you instead of meeting Ken and his friends. You should be mentoring the Kens of this world, not the other way around.'

Miriam smiled. 'We both know that's not how things work around here.'

'No kidding,' I sighed. 'Even the Peter Principle would be an improvement for the UN.'

She laughed as we walked to the security desk, where I returned my visitor badge and said goodbye to Miriam.

I walked a few steps out of the building and had to laugh, mainly at myself. What else could I really do? It was my own fault for agreeing to this meeting at the UN, and I swore to myself never to fall for it again – though the fifteen minutes with Miriam had made it all worthwhile.

Later that afternoon, I received an email from Lisa, thanking me again for the meeting and informing me that they would be in touch after they had a chance to brief Mr Dellin. Thirty-eight people were cc'd on her message.

Mr Dellin was not among them.

Luanda Lessons

The latest experience at the UN had taken the wind out of my sails. Even though I had gone into that meeting with my eyes wide open and disabused of any illusions, this massive organization had yet again managed to disappoint even the lowest of expectations. I remembered how Jacques would sneer every time I tried to put a positive spin on the UN and its potential for good. For him, the purpose of the UN had existed ever so briefly when it replaced the useless League of Nations at the end of the Second World War, and then run its course in the 1960s after international recognition of the newly independent states following the end of colonization. Ever since then, as Jacques liked to say, the inmates had been running the asylum.

I found myself forlorn and disoriented. It was time to find my way back to working directly with the people on the ground in Africa, rather than through international organizations and their giant bureaucracies. I resolved to drift back into my childhood for inspiration, with its vanished idyll, rather than get stuck in my frustration at the displays of institutional cluelessness and exercises in futility. They all amounted to a big fat nothing. I knew full well that for every Miriam there would be many, many Kens. The gems were few and far between. But each one was worth it.

A few weeks after the UN breakfast meeting, my Namibian friend Harald arranged for me to have a conversation with Congressman Jimmy Remerson, a prominent member of the United States House of Representatives. Harald was a wonderful person, a believer in the human spirit, an eternal optimist for no good reason. We had met in Harare a few months earlier and hit it off immediately. Harald had been deeply involved in the liberation movements in southern Africa, and had excellent connections with political leaders worldwide. Despite the ugly cynicism of Western politics when it came to supporting these struggles for liberation and independence, Harald harboured not an ounce of bitterness or resentment. And, as a man obsessed with twentieth-century European history, he never doubted that America was a force for good in the world, the last bastion of freedom.

Harald was convinced that our firm's work could make a difference in southern Africa. All the countries in the region could use this help, he repeated again and again. Above all, Angola.

Angola, Harald explained, had been shattered by decades of civil war kept alive by oil and diamond money, a country ravaged by disease and landmines, infiltrated by Cuban and South African mercenaries, experimenting with some bastardized version of Marxism while benefiting just an exclusive club of kleptocrats at the top. Independence, perhaps, but hardly liberation, or, as Harald liked to tell me, 'not yet Uhuru, to quote an astute Kenyan friend'. Basically, Angola was a really messed-up place.

Harald asked me whether I would be willing to meet with Congressman Remerson in his capacity as member of the House of Representatives' Subcommittee on Africa, to discuss Angola. Apparently, Congressman Remerson had expressed some interest in Angola at a recent conference, in which he had shared a discussion panel with Harald. I told Harald that I did not mind, and that he could give the Congressman my direct telephone number.

A few days later, my phone rang.

'Am I talking to Daniel Levin?' a pleasant voice asked.

'You are. Who's speaking, please?'

'This is Angie. I am calling from Congressman Remerson's office. Please hold for the Congressman.'

I was put on hold. After about thirty seconds of silence, I assumed the line had been disconnected and hung up. A minute later, my phone rang again.

'Why did you hang up?' Angie asked.

'I assumed we'd been disconnected,' I replied.

'Oh no,' Angie said. 'I was trying to put you through to Congressman Remerson. Please hold again for the Congressman.'

Again, I was put on hold. This time, I waited a minute and a half before hanging up. This was getting silly. Thirty seconds later, my phone rang again.

'What's going on, Daniel?' Angie asked.

'I don't know, Angie, you tell me. You call me because the Congressman supposedly wants to talk to me, but then I am put on hold, and nothing happens.'

'I'm so sorry, Daniel,' Angie said. 'The Congressman is very busy, and when he asks me to place the call, I have to do it immediately. Because he is dealing with several things at the same time, it's possible that it takes a moment or two for him to get on the line. I'm really sorry, that's how things work around here. When the President calls the Congressman, we sometimes end up waiting, too.'

It was the army principle, perfected in Washington. Someone above you stomps on your head, and you stomp on the head of the one below you. In politics it's called leadership.

'Anyway,' Angie continued. 'Can I put you through to the Congressman? He's standing right next to me.'

'Sure,' I said, hoping that Congressman Remerson had not listened to the entire exchange with Angie.

This time I waited no more than fifteen seconds before the Congressman jumped on the line.

'Hi, Daniel,' he said. 'Is it okay for me to call you Daniel?'

'Sure, Congressman,' I answered, wondering for a moment how he would have reacted if I had said no, or if I had called him by his first name.

'Well, Daniel, I don't have much time, but I did want to talk to you about Angola. My friend Harald mentioned to me that you do some interesting work in Africa, and that it could be very helpful to Angola.'

'That's very kind of Harald.'

'Yeah, he's a hell of a nice guy! One of the good ones. Anyway, as you may know, Angola is becoming increasingly important to us. How much do you know about Angola?'

'Well, I am aware of the civil war there, of America's support for Savimbi and his UNITA, and of the Soviet and Cuban support for the MPLA government. Also . . .'

'Yeah, yeah,' Remerson cut me off impatiently. 'Let's look forward, shall we? I'll cut right to the chase. Our subcommittee is supportive of a USAID project in Angola to develop their economy. Tell me, Daniel, how good is your French?'

'My French?' I asked, perplexed.

'Yeah, your French. After all, if you are going to do some work there, you'll have to communicate with the people around you.'

'I'm sorry, Congressman, but I don't think Angola was a French colo . . .'

'Yeah, yeah, whatever,' he interrupted me again, sounding more like a petulant teenager than a member of the United States Congress. 'Let's say you're right. So they speak English. That shouldn't present too much of a problem for you, right?'

'Actually, I think they mostly speak Portuguese, Congressman,' I said as mildly as I could. 'Angola used to be a Portuguese colony. Though I'm sure some people there do speak English.'

'Let me tell you something, son,' the Congressman said in a condescending tone, clearly annoyed that I had been wasting his time with my insolence. 'Where I come from, it's generally not considered a very good idea to correct a senior member of the United States Congress. I have to run to a meeting now. I'll talk to my guys at AID and ask them to give you a call. But before they do, you might want to read up on the country and get your history straight. Portuguese colony . . .!'

Congressman Remerson hung up without saying goodbye. I found myself holding the receiver, wondering what had just happened. I decided to call Harald and vent my frustration at him.

'So how did it go with Remerson?' Harald asked as he picked up. 'What is our situation?'

'Well,' I answered, 'to paraphrase a great yet flawed American president, it depends on what your definition of "is" is.'

'That bad?' Harald said after a short pause.

'Let's put it this way,' I replied, trying not to sound too disappointed, 'for a person who claims to be focused on Angola, and especially for a member of the House's Subcommittee on Africa, Congressman Remerson had a few minor knowledge gaps.'

I told Harald how the Congressman thought that Angola had been a French or a British colony, and how completely unaware he was of Portugal's colonial history in Angola.

Harald laughed. 'Too funny! I suppose a senior legislator of the only remaining superpower can afford to be clueless. Remerson didn't strike me as the sharpest tool in the shed, but I thought he could be helpful. Would you be willing to consider plan B?'

I wasn't in the mood for playful banter, still peeved at Remerson's distinctive combination of ignorance and arrogance. 'That depends on what plan B is. What do you have in mind?'

'Will you be in my neck of the woods anytime soon?' Harald asked.

'As a matter of fact, I plan to be in South Africa next week,' I said.

'Perfect,' Harald said. 'Let's meet over dinner and talk about Angola. I would like to introduce you to a friend in Sandton, who will be keen to meet you, and who could be very helpful.'

The following Tuesday evening, Harald picked me up in my hotel and we drove to the restaurant in Sandton where we would meet his friend Inácio. On the way he gave me an extensive briefing on Inácio, who had been a senior official in the Angolan government for many years. According to Harald, Inácio was a hardened veteran, old school, and had been playing an important role in Angola since the country's independence (yes, from Portugal . . .) in the mid-1970s. He had held many high positions in the economy and in foreign affairs, and from what Harald said, he was one of the good guys, relatively clean. I didn't press for a more precise definition of 'relatively'.

Inácio was waiting for us when we arrived at the restaurant. I took an instant liking to this man. He was pleasant and refined, and clearly extremely bright and experienced. The type of person who understood what I was saying halfway through my sentences. We talked about Angola, and about the need for capacity building and public education in order to create even a semblance of financial inclusion. Inácio understood immediately that for our efforts to succeed we would have to keep our initiative apolitical, somewhere in no man's land between the MPLA government and Savimbi's UNITA opposition. Since the MPLA controlled the oil and UNITA controlled the diamonds to fund their endless war, perhaps the financial sector could be the middle ground for some sane voices to meet, according to Inácio. Wishful thinking, perhaps, but crazier things have happened, as Harald put it, and if anyone could get that done it would be Inácio.

Over the next three months we discussed and planned the framework, contents, and budget of this initiative. Inácio proved to be very astute, and provided invaluable input not only on what we should do, but on how and to which people to present it in the capital, Luanda, in order for this ambitious project to see the light of day. We met once more at Inácio's home in Sandton, and he introduced me to a good friend of his, Aleixo, another former Angolan minister. Inácio and Aleixo explained to me their good cop–bad cop tactics for getting the initiative approved and funded by the Angolan government, and for keeping the vultures at a manageable distance.

I did not hear back from Inácio or Aleixo for over a month after the Sandton meeting, and was starting to give up on the Angolan project, when I received a fax from Aleixo. He informed me that we were all set, and that my visit to Luanda was being prepared.

The project called for our team to spend one week per month in Angola, working with a group of about fifty professionals and teaching them the fundamentals of financial and capital markets. Between each stay in Luanda, we put together extensive manuscripts in English and Portuguese, which we took with us in three enormous, heavy suitcases. A few months into the initiative, I was scheduled to travel to Luanda with Grace, one of our firm's associates, who had worked with me on preparing the particular topic and manuscript for that month. Two days before our departure, I received a telephone call from Inácio's son Gino, whom I had met during one of my previous stays in Luanda.

'Hello, Daniel, how's it hanging?' Gino asked. He spoke excellent English, but his attempts at slang tended to misfire.

'Everything is fine, Gino, we're getting ready for our next trip. Will you be in Luanda in the coming days?'

'I will. Actually, I was calling to ask you for a small favour. My Dad told me that you were expected in Luanda soon, and I wondered if you could bring me something I urgently need. Nothing major, don't worry,' Gino said.

'Sure, Gino, what is it you need?' I asked.

'Well, I have this Firebird here in Luanda. It's a real beauty, you know,' Gino said.

'Excuse me, what is it you have in Luanda?' I had no idea what he was talking about.

'A Firebird. You know, a Pontiac Firebird. Black as the night. Black trim, black leather. What can I say, Daniel, I just love my muscle cars. Guilty as charged.'

'Oh, okay, what about this car?' I asked, not sure where this conversation was heading.

'It needs, how shall I say, it needs a new fender,' Gino said.

'A new what?' I was sure that I had misheard him.

'A new fender,' Gino said. 'Don't you know what a car fender is?'

'I know what a car fender is. What I don't know is what you would like me to do. You want me to take a Pontiac Firebird fender on my flight from New York to Joburg and from Joburg to Luanda?'

'That's right,' Gino replied, as casually as if he had asked me to pick up a box of chocolates at the airport. 'The Firebird is a 1980 model. A beauty, as I told you. But the fender is shot, it needs to be replaced. I found this parts dealership in upstate New York that has one fender left for the 1980 model. I would appreciate if you could pick it up and bring it with you on this trip.'

For a moment, I was at a loss for words. 'But Gino, I don't think I can do that. I don't think the airline will just allow me to check in a car fender.'

'My Dad says you're a smart guy, I'm sure you'll figure it out,' Gino said. Evidently, in his twenty-two years, Gino had figured out a few things himself, including entitlement and condescension.

'Sorry, Gino, I don't think I can do that. We're scrambling to get the manuscripts ready, and there's no way I can organize your car fender and a cargo shipment before we leave.'

'That's too bad,' Gino said in the most arrogant tone possible for someone barely old enough to drive a car. 'This was not a question, Daniel. It was a request. Angola is all about relationships, as you will learn one day. This would have been a nice gesture towards our family.'

'I'll have to find a way to make it up to your family, Gino. I hope your father won't be too disappointed,' I said.

'Please leave my father out of this Firebird matter,' Gino shot back, his tone suddenly more pleasant. 'No need to drag him into this. I'm sure there will be ample opportunity for you to show your appreciation towards my father and the family.' Or, rather, as it seemed, the Family, with a capital F.

Gino evidently possessed all the ingredients for a successful politician. It was safe to assume that he didn't hear the word 'no' very often.

I had put this unpleasant Gino episode behind me when Grace and I and the three oversized suitcases arrived at JFK airport two days later. Poor Grace was scared to death of flying, and she was practically hyperventilating at the prospect of a sixteen-hour flight to Johannesburg. She had stocked up on all kinds of over-the-counter and not so over-the-counter pills. This was not the moment to explain that the truly miserable leg of the trip happened to be the Johannesburg–Luanda flight.

I fell asleep shortly after takeoff. When I woke up eight hours later, rejuvenated and relaxed, I looked at Grace and had a shock. Her face was white as a sheet, and clearly she was not feeling well. Apparently, as she told me not without bitterness, I had slept through the worst turbulences she had ever experienced. The plane had been shaking violently and dropped a few hundred feet several times. Grace told me that she had been sure we were all going to die. Even though the flight was smooth at this point, her hands were still clutching the sides of her seat in a death grip, white knuckles and all. My promise to make it up to her over dinner with a nice bottle of wine did not do much to improve her mood.

The arrival in Luanda at the hottest time of the day was the usual tropical treat: extreme heat and humidity, waiting for the shuttle bus at the bottom of the plane without a drop of shade, the stuffy queue at passport control that did not seem to move, praying that the police officer had woken up in a good mood that day and was satisfied with our immunization cards. The alternative meant a visit to the airport infirmary and a lengthy negotiation in Portuguese to avoid an unnecessary polio booster shot. Fortunately, twenty dollars were usually sufficient to remedy any medical shortcomings of our immunization cards.

Vaccinations were a sensitive subject for me, as the heavy doses of the anti-malaria drug Lariam – mefloquine – were starting to have some nasty side effects, from terrifying nightmares and hallucinations to toxic consequences for my liver. At my last medical checkup, the doctor had sternly advised me to stop drinking if I wanted to save what was left of my liver. Only after I swore to him that I was not an alcoholic did we figure out that it had been the constant intake of Lariam that had caused this problem. Since Lariam had to be taken one week before arrival in a malaria-risk region and for four weeks after leaving it, my monthly trips to Angola meant that I never got a break from this scary drug.

Our assistant António was waiting for us on the other side of passport control. António was a wonderful young man. He was very bright and helpful, spoke excellent English, and was permanently upbeat. During my stays in Luanda, António never left my side, and I always appreciated his insights and explanations. On many occasions I felt he was smarter and more knowledgeable than all the ministers and public officials we met.

António helped us with the three suitcases, two of which had taken a serious beating during the trip. The baggage area was stiflingly hot, and by the time we were in António's car Grace and I were drenched in sweat. I was craving a cold shower.

Our training session was scheduled to begin the next morning, and António asked me whether I would like to sit in on a World Bank seminar, which was taking place that afternoon at the National Bank, since we had a few hours to kill before dinner with Inácio, Aleixo, and their friends. I accepted António's offer, curious to see how the World Bank chose to do its teaching in Angola.

We arrived at the beautiful, pinkish colonial-era National Bank building about one hour into the seminar. I took a seat in the back of the room and waved discreetly to Brian Katter, the World Bank representative who was conducting the seminar. I had worked with Brian a few years earlier on a banking reform project and had come to appreciate him as a brilliant mathematician, socially a little awkward perhaps, but pleasant enough. Brian waved back to me, and continued his presentation. The topic of the afternoon was systemic risk in payment systems. There were about thirty people in attendance, half of whom seemed to be fast asleep, which didn't seem to bother Brian. He was advocating forcefully for the introduction of cutting-edge risk-management systems in the Angolan interbank market. On his overhead projector Brian explained the algorithms and formulae for instantaneous settlement cycles, multilateral netting, participant funds, and how all these measures would not only solve many of Angola's financial problems, but also make the country a worldwide pioneer in electronic payment systems. Forty-five minutes after I had arrived Brian announced a fifteen-minute coffee break, which seemed to awaken everyone in attendance. He came to the back of the room and we shook hands.

'Hello, Daniel,' he said with a smile. 'What a nice surprise to meet you here, of all places.'

'Hi, Brian, nice to see you.'

'I hope you enjoyed my presentation. What did you think of it?' Brian asked.

'Well, it was interesting,' I hedged carefully, hoping Brian would let me leave it at that.

'Interesting – good, or interesting – bad?' Brian wanted to know. 'Tell me honestly what you think. This is my first time in Angola, and I wasn't sure where to begin.'

'Well, for starters, it is safe to assume that no more than ten per cent of the audience understands English,' I said. 'So even if every one of those ten per cent was among the fifty per cent that stayed awake, you're essentially talking to three people.'

Brian was taken aback. 'I never even considered that. I should have asked for a translator, I suppose. But what did you think about the substance of my presentation? You must have appreciated it. After all, it's something you and I have discussed in the past.'

'You're right, we have,' I said. 'But we talked about this in the context of the New York Clearing House Association or the new screen-based exchange in Frankfurt. This is Luanda.'

'What do you mean?' Brian seemed genuinely perplexed by my observation.

'I mean that you can't compare Luanda to these sophisticated, highly developed financial markets. There, they worry about trying to limit the exposures in case the payment systems go down, and even the backup systems fail. Here in Angola, they have slightly different problems.'

'How are they different? A payment system is a payment system,' Brian said, rather definitively.

'Not really,' I replied. 'This is a place without reliable telephone lines, which means there are no electronic payment systems to speak of. This is an all-cash economy. Here, systemic risk means a bank gets robbed at gunpoint or a truckload of cash is stolen, or there is a fire in the National Bank.'

Brian went quiet. 'My goodness,' he said after a long pause, 'I never even considered that. I gave the same presentation in Abidjan, in Kinshasa, even in Bangui in the Central African Republic.'

'Probably with the same results,' I said, instantly regretting the fact that I was piling on this poor fellow.

'Probably,' Brian said, sounding very dejected. 'But if they have no idea what I am talking about, and especially if most of them don't understand English, why do they come? It must be pure torture for them! Why do they sit through this?'

'I don't know. Perhaps for the coffee and cookies. Or because this room is cooler than their workspace.'

'I feel a little bad now,' Brian said. 'What a waste of the World Bank's resources, wouldn't you say?'

'No argument here,' I replied. I couldn't think of a truthful retort to make him feel better.

'Well,' Brian said with a smile, 'at least I got an interesting trip out of this. Don't know if I'll get another chance to visit Angola. There are, you know, benefits in working for the World Bank. Can't say that our work is always terribly meaningful, but the pay is pretty good and you do get to travel the world and see some pretty exotic places. Perhaps,' he added after a short, reflective pause, 'these poor countries don't get much bang for their buck from the World Bank, but I sure do.'

We parted on that insightful note.

The next morning, António picked us up at our hotel for the short ride to the Ministry of Finance, which had an auditorium large enough to host our training session. The ministry building was bustling with people standing in line for licences and permits, or just visiting friends and relatives who were working there. This was the first time Grace would have to speak in front of a large group, and she was very nervous. Our translator Margarida tried to calm her down, assuring Grace that it would be helpful for her to have a simultaneous translation, since it gave her double the time to think about her next words. But the closer we got to the auditorium, the more nervous Grace became, finally stopping and grabbing my arm.

'I can't do this, Daniel,' she said. 'I think I'm having a panic attack.'

I tried to calm her down, without much success.

'Come on, Grace,' Margarida chimed in, 'when you're done today, we'll celebrate your maiden lecture with a gin and tonic. We'll leave Daniel in the hotel, and I'll take you to a nice place on the beach. It's beautiful there, and they even allow you to smoke. Just us girls. What do you say?'

'Actually, I could use a cigarette right now,' Grace said. She seemed completely zoned out.

Before Margarida and I could react, Grace pulled a pack of cigarettes out of her handbag and lit one, right there, smack in the hallway of the Ministry of Finance under a bright 'no smoking' sign. We were getting some strange, bewildered looks. At that very moment the Minister of Finance and the head of the National Bank were walking towards us.

'You might want to put that out,' I whispered.

'Oops, sorry,' Grace said, still with that strange blank look. She dropped her cigarette to the floor and stepped on it as it fell on the rug. 'Let's go inside.'

Margarida shrugged her shoulders, and we followed Grace into the auditorium.

The lecture session that morning was devoted to Adam Smith and his political economy. I considered Adam Smith to be the father of modern economics, and I loved his rational approach to liberty and free speech. After an introduction to *The Wealth of Nations*, spiced up with some anecdotes about Margaret Thatcher's infatuation with this book – supposedly, she always carried a copy in her handbag – and a brief discussion of Smith's often misquoted 'invisible hand' metaphor, I spent about ninety minutes talking about price formulation in a competitive market. I explained the interaction between supply and demand, the effect on price, how a price was likely to be high if the supply was low and the demand was high, and how, inversely, the price would be low if the supply was high and the demand was low. Margarida translated everything faithfully, and I was rather pleased with the way the morning session had gone. It was time to break for lunch. Grace told me that she was not sure she was up for delivering the afternoon lecture. I told her not to worry about it, and that I would do her part if she still felt that way after lunch.

As I was collecting my notes, Inácio walked up to the podium.

'That was well done, Daniel, very interesting,' he said with a smile.

'Thank you, Inácio,' I replied. 'I'm glad you enjoyed it. It was nice of you to come and offer moral support.'

'It's the least I can do. By the way, Gino mentioned to me that the two of you had a slight misunderstanding. Nothing serious, he said. Is everything okay?'

I wasn't expecting that. I liked Inácio and didn't want to rehash the spat with Gino, whom I considered to be nothing more than a spoiled brat.

'I suppose it was a slight misunderstanding, yes, one could call it that,' I said. 'Nothing serious, as Gino put it.'

'Well, Daniel,' Inácio said as he put his hand on my shoulder, 'I know that Gino can be a little difficult at times, and I hope he didn't inconvenience you. But remember that he is on very good terms with the President's children, especially his daughter. It would be wise to give Gino what Gino wants.'

'I'll keep that in mind, Inácio,' I replied. This conversation seemed straight from *The Godfather*, Angola-style.

As we headed out of the auditorium, the local TV station asked me for a short interview, which I gladly agreed to. Grace told me that she wanted to go back to the hotel to rest and prepare for the afternoon session, and António kindly offered to drop her off and return to pick me up at the end of the interview.

Twenty minutes later, António was back, perfectly timed as the interview was concluding. It had gone well, and I was in a good mood. As we headed to the car, António asked me whether I was up for something different, for a change.

'What do you have in mind?' I asked him.

'Let me surprise you,' António replied.

We drove for about half an hour to the outskirts of Luanda and entered an area I wasn't familiar with. The crowded streets were bustling with people, many of whom seemed to be in heated discussions.

'Where are we?' I asked António.

'This is Luanda's black market,' he said. 'I wanted to show you this place. It is run by two Lebanese families. You can buy anything you need here, and everything is traded with everything. You can trade bread for eggs, milk for paper, paper for pants, shoes for bicycles, and so on. There is a central location where all the prices are listed, and where they are updated throughout the day. A huge chalkboard, operated by the administrator of this market.'

I was stunned. This market was one giant goods and commodities exchange where everything was bartered, an entire city in itself. I had never seen anything like it. My face was glued to the car window as we drove slowly through the narrow streets.

'I listened carefully to your lecture this morning,' António continued. 'It was very interesting. I think I get it: if you have a lot of one item relative to the demand, the price for that item will go down. And I get the opposite, too. And I think most people here get it, too. I thought I would show you this place.'

I was mesmerized by the happenings on the street. It felt like a giant exchange floor, but surprisingly well organized, not chaotic at all.

'This is just incredible,' I said. 'I had no idea such a place existed.'

'This place has been here for many years,' António said. 'It has thrived during the worst war years, when Savimbi was butchering people left and right. And it has thrived during calmer, more peaceful periods.'

'Just incredible,' I repeated. 'Amazing.'

'Would you like to take a stroll, have a closer look?' António asked.

'Can we?' I wondered.

António laughed. 'But of course. This is not Detroit. It's safe here. Believe me, there is no safer place in Luanda. Everyone here is too focused on making money to be distracted by crime. I think Adam Smith would have approved.'

I smiled. Clearly, I had nothing to teach this man.

António stopped the car in an alley next to a large building that looked like a warehouse, and we got out.

'Come, Daniel, let me show you something.'

We stepped into the building. Inside, there were at least two hundred people, busily shouting numbers and running from person to person with little scraps of paper. There were six giant blackboards in the centre of the hall, forming a perfect hexagon. Each blackboard seemed to have four people keeping track of changing prices. The blackboards were divided into separate categories of goods and foods, and the prices were continuously updated. It was an incredible display of pure market forces. My mouth was wide open.

'Are you okay?' António asked.

'I'm speechless, António. I don't know what to say. I have never seen anything like this. These people are extraordinary, this place is remarkable. I have no words.'

António smiled. 'The trading is in their blood. They know about supply and demand, and they know when a price is right, or efficient, as you called it this morning. What they don't know, and what they really do need to learn from you, is a way to formalize all this, to legalize it, regulate it. Not sure I am using the right term, but I think you understand what I mean. Angola lacks the legal framework for all this. The rule of law. This is what everyone here really craves. The rule of law.'

I didn't answer. I felt like such a fool. Here I was, all grandiose and pretentious, teaching these young Angolans about supply and demand, when clearly each and every one of them could have taught me quite a bit about that. And to think that I had been so dismissive of Brian Katter and his World Bank nonsense on payment systems!

António interrupted my mental self-flagellation. 'I would like to introduce you to someone, Daniel, if you don't mind.'

We walked to the corner of the hall, where there was a segregated area. A beautiful young lady came towards us and gave António a kiss.

'Daniel, this is my wife Rosa. Rosa, this is my boss Daniel, whom I had mentioned to you.'

Rosa stretched out her hand and smiled. 'Very pleased to meet you, sir,' she said in perfect English.

'The pleasure is all mine, Rosa. Please call me Daniel.' And looking at António, I added: 'Perfect English and also beautiful!'

'We met at the university,' Rosa answered for António, ignoring my compliments. 'I was studying English, and António economics and finance. I ended up working in this market, and António works as an interpreter. As the saying goes: man – or woman – plans, and God laughs.'

'Indeed,' I said. 'The same could be said for the way I planned today's lecture. God will be laughing for a while, if He managed to stay awake. Tell me, Rosa, if you don't mind, what exactly do you do here?'

'Well, it's difficult to explain, at least for me,' Rosa replied. 'It's complicated. I run a side-board in this market that allows people to sell goods they don't yet own. As I said, they don't own these goods, but they are promised to be delivered. Actually, I am the one who lends them the goods from someone else's inventory. When the goods are sold, they are credited to the seller's account, which I track on this board, and I force them to buy back the goods and return them to me, so that I can pass it back to the other person's inventory. I apologize if it sounds more complicated than it is. In fact, it's a really neat thing, because it allows the first person essentially to bet that the price for the goods will go down. When that price drops, the person can buy back the goods at a lower price. The difference is the profit on the bet. Sorry for being so long-winded.'

I was completely flabbergasted. What Rosa had just described to me, and had done so in a far more articulate manner than I would have been capable of, was the short selling of these goods. It was absolutely brilliant!

'Are you kidding me, Rosa?' I exclaimed. 'You are shorting these goods! This is simply magnificent. Incredible! You guys are geniuses.'

'You are too kind, Daniel,' Rosa said. 'I don't know what that word means, shorting. In fact, we have a lot to learn. António told me about your lectures, and I wish I could take part. But someone in this family has to be the breadwinner,' she added with a playful wink at António.

'No, Rosa,' I said. 'I am the one doing all the learning today. This is fascinating. You are engaging in very sophisticated trading. Where do you make your money in this?'

'Well, there are several aspects that turn out a nice profit,' Rosa replied, a little sheepishly. 'I charge a modest fee for lending the goods, or rather for arranging the lending of the goods, from the other person's inventory. It's sort of a rental fee. Of course I make sure that this modest fee is a little less modest than the modest fee I pay the owner of the inventory. The difference might not be that large, but so many people are asking to place these bets that the prices will drop, so it adds up to a nice little profit for us.'

'This is brilliant,' I said. 'You should have been delivering this morning's lecture on supply and demand, and on the way a price is determined. You know infinitely more about this topic than I do.'

'Oh, no,' Rosa said, blushing. 'Actually, I sometimes get the sense that we're playing with fire. I feel that people are seduced too easily by these bets, and that all this could come crashing down. In fact, it seems that the bets themselves – the shorting, as you call them – make the prices of the goods go down.'

'A self-fulfilling prophecy,' António jumped in.

'Something like that,' Rosa continued. 'I feel like all this shorting needs more supervision. For example, I feel like someone should be forced to own the goods outright before betting on them. It should not be enough to bet on a rental, if you know what I mean. But I probably don't know what I am talking about. Forgive me.'

'Quite the opposite, Rosa,' I said. 'You have completely nailed it. Based only on your experience and your intelligence, you have identified the soft spot and the risks of shorting. I cannot tell you how impressed I am.' Turning to António, I added: 'You are a very lucky man.'

'I know,' António said with a smile. 'But if you pay Rosa any more compliments, my life will become unbearable. It's already hard enough to keep up with her.'

All three of us laughed. It was time to head back, since traffic in Luanda was atrocious, and we still had to pick up Grace and return to the Ministry of Finance for the afternoon session. Rosa stayed professional – no hugs or kisses, just a firm handshake – and wished me all the best with her compatriots. 'By the time you are done teaching the Angolans, you will either love or hate this place,' she said. 'Here, there is not much room in between those two sentiments.'

On the drive back I was in a pensive state of mind and didn't speak much. I felt humbled, even embarrassed, by what I had just experienced. Fresh off my grandiose lecture on finance and economics, I had received a humbling lecture of my own. And what a lecture it had been! What had started as a presumption of my knowledge and the Angolans' ignorance had ended in the realization of their knowledge and my ignorance. Rosa, with all her charm and professionalism, had managed to hold a mirror up to me and make me take a long, hard look at myself. It wasn't a pretty sight.

António seemed to read my thoughts. 'Don't be so hard on yourself,' he said gently. 'Hundreds of so-called experts from the World Bank, the IMF, the African Development Bank, come through here. Hundreds of advisers from NGOs such as the Ford Foundation, and hundreds of superstars from outfits like McKinsey. They all come here assuming that they will be enlightening the natives, teaching us how to eat with a fork and knife, how to say "Yes, sir" and "No, sir". Some are pleasant, and some are arrogant and condescending. But all of them are comically clueless about Angola, its history, its culture, its politics, and especially its people.'

I remained silent as António navigated around the mammoth potholes in the streets. If slalom driving had been an Olympic sport, Angola would have flat-out owned this discipline.

'All these experts assume we know nothing about money, about capitalism,' António continued. 'These people probably think the Soviets also knew nothing about capitalism, and that the Chinese today don't either, just because these regimes call themselves communists. In fact, the opposite is true. Nobody today is more capitalist than the Chinese. Money is their religion. Compared to them, America is a socialist nation. If you want to see true capitalism in action, look at countries like Angola, with abject poverty and a huge wealth gap. Believe me, that is where people have no choice but to understand how money works. When you have so little, you don't need lectures on the value of money or on the price of things. We get that.'

António's words felt like an ice-cold shower. Everything he said was one hundred per cent true. He didn't sound angry. He spoke calmly and in a very matter-of-fact manner.

'I know,' I said meekly. 'I know now. I will have to rethink my approach to the lectures here.'

'Actually,' António said, 'you don't have to change all that much, only the focus and the perspective. We still need to learn about these things, but mainly because we need to formalize our economy. And what we need the most are the tools to do this ourselves. We don't want to rely on outside experts who come here and give the same speeches they gave last week in Kuala Lumpur or Lima or Kathmandu. As I said, we need the tools, and we need considerable help building the infrastructure of this country – the institutions, the legal and regulatory framework, you know, all that. But we should do it ourselves. And if we make mistakes, let us make our own mistakes. No need to import other people's mistakes. In fact, we're pretty good at making our own.'

'António, you should be the one to deliver this afternoon's lecture, not me or Grace,' I said.

'Oh no,' António said with a hearty laugh. 'I'm just the driver and part-time translator. And remember, despite everything I just said, in our country good advice is only worth something if it's perceived as coming from the outside. It's a branding thing, I suppose.'

'Perhaps you're right,' I said. 'But I really wish I had been aware of this before the lectures. I should have spoken to people on the ground first, to people like you and Rosa.'

'It's strange,' António said. 'There are plenty of fact-finding missions here. In fact, most of the time that is all the consultants do. They call it the diagnostic phase of their project. But there never is a next phase. Everything begins and ends with a standard report on poverty reduction and the need for financial education. I'm not kidding! And my personal favourite is the mandatory chapter in their brilliant diagnostic reports that laments the "corrosive effect of corruption". They all even use the same wording. I think they are basically cannibalizing each other's reports.'

An accident had forced traffic to a complete standstill. António was not pulling any punches. The strange thing was that he was continuing to speak in this tranquil, dispassionate voice, devoid of any anger or bitterness.

'Well, corruption is a big problem,' I said, not very convincingly.

'Of course it is,' António said. 'We get that, trust me. When you leave, we are the ones who are left to cope with the thieves at the top. Our elite wrote the handbook on corruption. But what good is it just to regurgitate the usual platitudes in these reports? Don't you think it's safe to conclude by now that criminalizing corruption has not worked all that well? Why not try something new? How about creating incentives for good behaviour by political leaders and their privileged minions? I mean, they already have all the money in the world. What they really crave is recognition by the West. Make that dependent on good – or let's just settle for "less disastrous" – behaviour. Why not make that recognition dependent on reaching some modest milestones? You know, nothing too ambitious, just a few roads and schools, maybe a vaccination programme here and there, clearing some landmines, feeding a few kids, cleaning some of the water. Nothing too demanding, Heaven forbid. Wouldn't be fair to expect too much.'

I really had nothing to teach this man, and everything to learn from him. In fact, I had learned more in the last hour than in the past ten years.

'Please tell me, António,' I said, 'what made you decide to take me on this excursion?'

António took a moment before he answered. Traffic had started to move again slowly, like a viscous liquid between the buildings.

'You were the first one I took to this market,' he said. 'You have been a little different from the others. Maybe it's because you grew up in Kenya, I don't know. You have always been more interested in our culture, in our people. I appreciated the fact that you made the effort to learn some Portuguese since you have been coming here.'

'Oh please,' I interrupted him. 'My Portuguese is so bad that it is more likely to get me in trouble than to help me.'

'Perhaps,' he laughed, 'I won't lie to you. It is pretty bad. Most of the time you may think it's Portuguese, but it's actually more like pidgin Spanish. But you made the effort. Some people in your lectures told me that you even tried to greet them in Umbundu. Believe me, Daniel, these things don't go unnoticed.'

'Glad to see that my self-humiliation was worth it,' I said.

'It was. And last time you were here, I saw you boogie to some Angolan music,' António said with a laugh. 'Bonga and Waldemar Bastos, if I remember correctly.'

'Oh, yeah, I remember, it was last month during our stay here, when we had some drinks at Cenário. The music was fantastic.'

'It is, though personally, I prefer classical music. But you are in good company – Rosa is a huge fan of Waldemar Bastos. Though, and I hope this doesn't offend you, your dancing could use some work.'

I laughed out loud. António was hardly wrong in his assessment.

'I'm not offended at all,' I said. 'A South African friend of mine likes to tease me by saying that Thabo Mbeki and I are the only two Africans without rhythm.'

António laughed so hard that the car swerved and almost hit a moped rider. 'You see, Daniel, that is why I took you on this excursion, and none of the others,' he said. 'Because you have not yet been completely ruined. All hope is not yet lost with you.'

We arrived in front of the hotel, where Grace was waiting for us. António and I were still laughing when we pulled up, and Grace gave me a strange look.

'Everything okay?' she asked, with a slight irritation in her voice.

'Everything very much okay,' I replied. 'We just had a lovely lunch break. How are you feeling?'

'I'm fine, ready to do some teaching,' Grace said.

'About that teaching,' I said. 'There are a few things I believe we may want to do a little differently.'

The rest of our stay was a blur. I decided to rethink our approach to these training weeks in a radical way, not only as far as the content of our lectures was concerned, but – more importantly – with respect to the entire methodology. No more assumptions that people on the ground knew nothing, and that we were enlightening them by our mere presence.

At the end of the week, António drove us to the airport. When we parted, he handed me a small, gift-wrapped package.

'What is this?' I asked.

'A small gift from Rosa. She asked me to give it to you when you leave.'

'That is incredibly kind of her, please thank her from me.'

'Of course. I look forward to seeing you next month. Have a safe trip.'

'Thank you, António. Thank you for everything.'

I gave António a big hug, and Grace and I walked into the departure terminal.

After we checked in, we proceeded to the security check. In front of us was an Angolan couple, dressed to kill. Each had a Louis Vuitton bag and carry-on suitcase. For some reason the security officer asked them to open their luggage, and a huge argument ensued. The couple refused to open the bags and suitcases, and threatened the poor officer and his family with all kinds of apocalyptic consequences because of his impertinence. Finally, the supervising officer arrived at the scene and managed to calm everyone down. He explained to the couple that it was security protocol to open random bags, and that theirs had the bad luck of being chosen. After some more screaming and shouting, the couple finally consented and signalled to the junior officer that he could open their bags. What I saw next just flat-out shocked me: each bag and suitcase was stuffed to the brim with one hundred dollar bills. There must have been millions of dollars in there! I looked at Grace, who was staring at the cash in frozen horror. But the craziest part of the whole scene was the nonchalance with which the security officer asked the couple to close their bags and proceed to passport control, as if he was witnessing such situations routinely many times a day. Business as usual at Luanda's Quatro de Fevereiro airport.

António was right: the Angolans had nothing left to learn about capitalism and the value of money.

In the plane, I realized that I had forgotten to open Rosa's gift. I pulled it out of my bag and unwrapped it. It was a used paperback book – *O Caminho da Servidão* – the Portuguese translation of F. A. Hayek's iconic *The Road to Serfdom*. There was a small note inside the book: 'Remember, Daniel: we cannot teach anybody anything. We can only make them think. If that's good enough for Socrates, it sure is good enough for us! Warmest wishes, Rosa'.

Escape from Dakar

I could not get António and Rosa out of my head. Interacting with them had been inspiring, but the experience had still left me exhausted by the daunting prospect of having to rethink and re-calibrate our entire approach to development. Perhaps it was no different from what Mark Grant had told me on my first day at his law firm – that I would learn more from the legal assistants and the secretaries and the cleaning crew than I would from the most senior, revered partners at the firm. For all his flaws, Mark did appreciate those who were most habitually overlooked, and he realized that they often had more to teach us than the big shots.

It was time for me to talk less and listen more. What I might have possessed in knowledge, I lacked in understanding. Perhaps there was less separating me from the likes of UN Ken than I had thought. My professional world had been turned upside down. I was con-fused and craved a break. I wanted to clear my mind, empty my cup, so a trip to Paris came just at the right time. I had loved the city ever since I lived there in the mid-1990s, and tried to return whenever I could.

Even though I had vowed to myself that I would take a few days off, a close friend from Morocco convinced me to meet a Gambian diplomat during my stay in Paris. A day later, I found myself in the lounge of the Hôtel de Crillon with this very distinguished-looking and charming Gambian ambassador, who listened attentively to my description of our work in Africa.

'You have to meet my President and tell him everything you've just told me,' the ambassador said. 'Everything. What you are describing is *exactly* what my country needs. I want to fly you to Banjul and meet with President Jammeh. Please.'

Apparently, the ambassador had been mandated by his President to locate people who could assist his country, the Gambia, in developing its economy and political system. I was already a little sceptical about the economic development part, but the desire to reform the political system really did strain credulity. President Jammeh was hardly known as a keen political reformer ever since taking power in a military coup in 1994.

The ambassador seemed to read my thoughts. 'Don't believe everything you hear and read,' he said. 'The Gambia and President Jammeh have been maligned for years. Yes, it is a poor country, and yes, it is a small country. But President Jammeh has a vision. He has a plan. Actually, he has several plans. He has a five-year plan, a ten-year plan, and a twenty-five-year plan.'

'No fifty-year plan?' I asked, tongue-in-cheek.

'Oh no, the President has no intention of staying in power for fifty years,' he answered, without a trace of sarcasm. Apparently, as long as the horizon was set at no longer than twenty-five years, the President had every intention of sticking around for a while. The ambassador planned to be right there with his boss for the duration of his reign.

'I don't know, Mr Ambassador,' I said, deciding to play it straight. 'As interesting as it would be, I must confess that I have my doubts regarding the leadership's willingness to reform the political system in the Gambia. We're quite busy at the moment, and I'm hesitating to pull our resources from other projects, if I am not convinced that we are dealing with a motivated decision-maker in Banjul.'

'Fair enough, sir, I understand,' the ambassador replied. 'I should also mention that the ADB is supportive of any sustainable initiative in the Gambia. They really want to see something succeed there, for a change.'

The African Development Bank. That was all I needed! If the World Bank could be painful to work with, the ADB took it to an entirely different level. Describing that experience as psychotic inefficiency on steroids would still be an understatement. After a particularly ridiculous experience about one year earlier, I had sworn to myself never again to get near the ADB. Agreeing now to work with the ADB once more would have satisfied Einstein's definition of insanity – repeating the same mistake, and expecting a different outcome.

'Dear Mr Ambassador,' I said. 'With all due respect, mentioning the ADB does not help your case.'

'I understand,' he replied. 'How about you fly to Banjul for one day only, meet my President, and then decide. All I ask is that you keep an open mind. And if you still wish to decline after meeting President Jammeh, at least you will have had an interesting adventure in West Africa.'

Neither of us had any idea how true those last words would prove to be.

I told the ambassador that I would get back to him within a few days. Perhaps I had been too quick to dismiss the strongman of this small African country. After all, my entire source of information had come from second-hand media reports, which generally recycled each other. I spoke to some friends in Africa, but none of them had been to the Gambia themselves, and they all only knew more or less what I knew. I called my Moroccan friend who had introduced me to the Gambian ambassador, and asked him to give me his honest thoughts.

'Well, Daniel,' he replied a little coyly, 'I suppose Switzerland or Norway are not exactly kicking in your front door, begging you to help them develop their economy or political system, right? You always told me that the more messed up a country was, the more interesting the challenge was to you. Well, the Gambia should be plenty interesting.'

He had a point. But there had to be a minimal degree of genuine interest and commitment on behalf of the ruler for our work to be effective.

'Sure, Mohamed,' I said, 'you're right. A country has to need what we have to offer. I don't doubt that the Gambia could use our help. I just don't have all that much faith in the ambassador's assurances about President Jammeh's degree of interest and commitment. It's hard to do this if I'm more motivated than the decision-maker on the ground. I'm not sure what to believe.'

'Listen, Daniel,' Mohamed shot back a little sharply. 'You're trying to change the minds of difficult people. People who are sometimes corrupt, sometimes cruel, usually indifferent to their nations' suffering, and almost always inept at governing. You're worried about what to believe? Let me make it easy for you: don't believe anything. Politicians lie. They do it everywhere, in Africa, in Asia, in Europe, in America, everywhere. Sometimes they believe their own lies, sometimes they don't. But they *always* believe that they are the saviours of their nations. They believe they are essential, and the most dangerous of them even believe they are immortal. Seriously, Daniel. You want to talk to me about two-faced politicians? This is my daily life, the bane of my existence. We have a saying: you don't teach an orphan how to cry. Don't talk to me about lying politicians. Go to the Gambia, or don't go to the Gambia. But if you go, don't expect paradise.'

Mohamed was right. The odds of a meaningful initiative in the Gambia were clearly long. Obviously. But this was exactly the kind of country we were targeting, and it was pointless to ask more questions. I called the ambassador and told him that I had decided to give it a shot and go to Banjul. He was delighted and after a brief exchange of phone calls we agreed on a date. He told me that everything would be taken care of, my accommodations, the VIP pickup at the airport, everything. There was no need for a visa, as the President's chief of protocol would pick me up at the plane. By the time we had worked it all out, I was actually looking forward to this trip.

The fastest route to Banjul was a flight with Air Afrique from New York to Dakar, and then another Air Afrique flight from Dakar to Banjul. The stopover in Senegal would be just ninety minutes, quite convenient. Our travel agent told us that Air Afrique guaranteed the connection, meaning that the flight from Dakar to Banjul would wait if the flight from New York happened to be late.

By the time the departure day arrived, I was pretty relaxed about the whole Gambia trip and President Jammeh. Check-in at JFK was smooth, though they told me that the airline's system did not allow them to issue the boarding pass for the second leg of the trip from Dakar to Banjul, and that I would have to do that at the transfer desk in Dakar. The flight left New York on time, and I fell asleep almost immediately.

I woke up an hour before we landed in Dakar and got my coffee fix. As we touched down, I noticed a burned-out plane to the right of the runway. Probably a training plane for fire drills and other emergencies, just like the one next to the runway in Zurich, I thought. The landing was smooth.

After leaving the plane, I hurried to locate a monitor for the connecting flight to Banjul. I could not find the transfer desk. Just before immigration, I finally saw the monitor, and immediately my heart sank. Next to the Air Afrique flight to Banjul, the word CANCELLED stared at me in thick, bold letters. I got hold of an airport agent and asked him what had happened to that flight.

'Did you see the burned plane next to the runway when you landed?' he asked me.

'I did. What about it?'

'That was your Air Afrique flight to Banjul. It missed the runway in a crash-landing one week ago and caught fire. By some miracle, nobody was seriously hurt, but the plane was destroyed. *Foutu*, as we say.'

I was stunned. How could they not have known that in New York in the days prior to the departure, or at the very least when I checked in?

'So what do I do now?' I asked the agent.

'Well, sir, you cannot really stay in this spot,' he said. 'You have to go through passport control, and then deal with your situation at the Air Afrique ticket office in the arrivals area.'

I thanked him and got in line for passport control. Only one booth was manned, and I counted thirty people in line ahead of me. It took the police officer about three minutes to check each passport, so I wrapped my mind around the fact that I would be standing in line for about one and a half hours.

Finally, I reached the front of the line and handed my passport to the officer. He looked at my picture, then at me, then again at my picture, then again at me. Finally, he shook his head.

'Sir, we have a problem,' the officer said. 'You have just attempted to enter Senegal without a visa, which is illegal. Come with me, please.'

The officer left his booth and walked away, signalling me to follow him. I heard a lot of cursing in the line behind me.

The officer took me to his supervisor, handed him my passport, and whispered a few words. They both looked at me, and then whispered a few more words. The supervisor signalled for me to approach.

'I see you are Swiss. Do you speak French?' he asked in a surprisingly pleasant tone.

'I do,' I replied. 'What's going on?'

'My friend, what is going on is that you have attempted to enter our country without a visa. As my colleague already informed you, that is not legal. We Senegalese consider that act a violation of our sovereignty.'

'I can assure you, officer,' I replied, trying my best not to laugh, 'that I have zero intention of violating your sovereignty. I never planned to enter Senegal. I was supposed to be in transit here on my way to Banjul.'

'That may be the case,' he replied, not unkindly. 'But you should not have tried to enter our country. You should have stayed in the transit area and waited for your next flight.'

'But I was told by an airport employee to go through passport control and deal with my situation at the Air Afrique ticket office in the arrivals area.'

'My Swiss friend,' he said with a pitying look, 'there is no Air Afrique office in the arrivals area. And now, we have a problem. A big problem. A very big problem, which we need to resolve. Please come with me.'

We walked back through the passport control area towards the transit zone. It seemed like the line had not moved one bit since I left it, and the people who were standing there were staring at me. The supervisor took me to a windowless office and beckoned the person in there to come to him. They exchanged a few words, and the supervisor turned to me.

'My Swiss friend,' he said, 'I am afraid you are under arrest. I will call headquarters to see what to do with you. In the meantime, our friend here will take care of you. Pierre is the warden of the airport prison.'

'You're joking, right?' I said, a little louder than intended.

'Oh no, my Swiss friend,' the supervisor replied, his tone still pleasant and calm. 'I never joke about such serious matters. I have to ask you to be patient, and we will figure out how to deal with this.'

'I would like to call the Swiss ambassador, if you don't mind,' I said. My cell phone didn't have a signal.

'There will be time for that, my friend,' he replied. 'In the meantime, I will leave you in Pierre's capable hands.'

Without waiting for my reply, he turned around and walked away. I looked at Pierre. He was a large fellow, in his late sixties or early seventies.

'Come with me, my friend,' Pierre said pleasantly. 'Let me take you to your detention cell, until a solution is found.'

For a fleeting moment I considered just walking away and talking myself onto the next Air Afrique flight back to New York. But I realized that the supervisor still had my passport. I wasn't going anywhere. For now, I was stuck in this absurd predicament.

I followed Pierre past a food court and a newspaper stand, into a small office on the other side of the airport terminal. He opened a door to a room, which had a desk and two chairs, and a small sink. Through the window, I saw the tarmac.

'This will be your cell for now, my friend,' Pierre said. 'I need to leave for a moment, but will be back soon. Can I get you anything to drink?'

If nothing else, Dakar airport did seem to have the friendliest police officers in the world. Pierre's kindness felt good.

'That's very nice of you,' I said. 'A cup of coffee would be lovely.'
'How do you take your coffee?' Pierre asked. 'Milk, sugar?'
'A little milk, please. Thank you.'

Pierre closed the door and locked it from outside. I sat at the desk with my head in the palms of my hands. This whole experience felt surreal, grotesque. Here I was, being detained by the airport police in Dakar, because my ongoing flight was cancelled and I had no legal place to be while I figured out how to leave. My situation was so absurd that it felt more comical than threatening. I was exhausted and closed my eyes.

I awoke to the sound of a key turning in the lock. Pierre stepped into the room with a warm smile. In one hand he had a steaming cup of coffee, and in the other hand he was holding a large bowl.

'I realized that you must be hungry,' he said, as he handed me the coffee, 'so I brought you some food.'

'That is very kind of you, thank you,' I answered. 'What is it?'

'A typical Senegalese dish called Thiéboudienne. Try it. If you like it, I will make sure you are immediately made an honorary citizen of Senegal, and then all your visa problems will be solved.'

Pierre laughed so hard at his joke that he started to cough and almost dropped the bowl. There was something contagious about this man's good humour, and soon enough we were both laughing our heads off in this small airport prison.

The coffee was black, strong, and sweet. The 'milk, no-sugar' part had apparently got lost in the process. I took a bite of the reddish food. It had a wonderful flavour.

'This is delicious, what is in it?' I asked.

'Just fish and rice, with some herbs and vegetables,' Pierre said. 'Bon appétit.'

My mood was improving. Strong coffee, delicious food, nice company – life wasn't all that bad. Pierre sat down and we started to talk about our families, jobs, politics, and music. It turned out that he was a huge jazz fan – his favourites were John Coltrane – 'has there ever been a better piece than "Blue Train"?' – and Miles

Davis – 'look up the word "cool" in the dictionary, and you will find a picture of Miles Davis'. Pierre's company made me relax and forget that I was actually imprisoned. After three hours, I asked to use the toilet. Pierre called his colleague and asked him to take me there, while he would check on my situation. For a short moment I again wondered whether I should make a run for it, but since I really had nowhere to run and was still passportless, I quickly dropped the idea.

Back in my cell, I went to the window and watched the planes on the tarmac. Just in front of the building there was an old single-engine Cessna 152. It seemed to be in pretty bad shape, the side doors were missing, and in their place there was some flimsy netting. During my university years I had learned to fly on this type of plane (with side doors). As I was checking out this banged-up specimen, Pierre entered the cell.

'Do you happen to know anything about that plane?' I asked him.

'Actually, yes, my friend,' Pierre replied. 'Believe it or not, this is my buddy's plane. He flies mail and packages to remote locations.'

'This is a postal plane?' I probed. 'Are you sure? The plane looks like it has seen better days.'

'Oh no, my friend,' Pierre said, 'quite the contrary. My buddy has been flying this plane for years and has never had an accident. He used to be an air force pilot and has seen it all. Trust me, this guy knows what he is doing. He flies everywhere.'

'Too bad he doesn't fly to the Gambia,' I said on a whim.

'Who says he doesn't, my friend?' Pierre shot back. 'He flies to Banjul and back twice a week.'

'He does?' I said. 'Too bad he can't take me with him.'

Pierre was silent for a moment. Then a mischievous smile crept on his face.

'Who says he can't?'

'Are you being serious?' I asked.

'My friend, nothing is impossible,' Pierre said, the same devilish smile still working its magic. 'It all depends on the right circumstances.'

'The right circumstances?' I probed.

'Yes, the right circumstances, my friend.'

Things were about to get interesting. I assumed that with 'circumstances' Pierre meant money, but I hesitated to engage him on this point out of fear that I might be rearrested for bribing a police officer. I had no desire to explore the inner workings of the Senegalese penitentiary system any further.

'Any chance you could be a little more specific?' I asked Pierre, who must have read my thoughts.

'Don't worry, my friend, we are just talking in hypotheticals, right?' he said with a laugh. 'No harm in discussing a business transaction, right? Hypothetically speaking, of course.'

'I suppose not,' I said. 'Hypothetically speaking, among old friends.'

Pierre moved his chair around the desk and sat next to me.

'Let's think this through, my friend,' he said, his voice noticeably lower than usual. 'My buddy has been flying this plane for years. He loves to fly, but I also know that he has a hard time making ends meet based on his meagre salary from the postal service. In fact, I suspect he will have to stop soon and look for a different job that pays more, perhaps in the construction business or in mining. If, on the other hand, there was a way to supplement his income ever so slightly, my buddy could continue to live his passion and fly the plane, and at the same time the Republic of Senegal would be able to retain this valuable public servant in its postal service. This means that by supplementing his income, hypothetically speaking, of course, we could kill two birds with one stone: helping out a good man, and at the same time fulfilling our patriotic duty of supporting the Senegalese civil service.'

Pierre was clearly liking the words coming out of his mouth. His voice was no longer low, and he stood up and started to pace.

'The more I think of it,' he continued, 'by helping out our buddy, you could atone for your shameful attempt to enter this country illegally. Your wrongful actions would be nullified, and instead you would be redeemed and celebrated, my friend.'

For appropriate emphasis, Pierre pounded the desk with his fist as he spoke the last words. I decided to go for it and strike while the iron was hot.

'So what would you consider an appropriate amount for me to fulfil this patriotic duty to the great nation of Senegal?' I asked.

'That depends, my friend,' Pierre replied, suddenly all business. 'How much cash do you have on you?'

'About five hundred dollars,' I said.

'Okay, not that much, but enough to show your dedication to the Republic of Senegal,' Pierre said with a slightly disappointed look. 'You will need to keep one hundred for yourself, so I would say two hundred for my buddy, and two hundred for me. In the spirit of our transaction, I will give it to a deserving charity. An orphanage, maybe.'

I tried to avoid eye contact with Pierre in order to keep a straight face. I pulled out my wallet, counted four hundred dollars, and handed the money to Pierre.

'Pleasure doing business with you,' I said.

'Don't think of it as business, my friend,' Pierre replied. 'Today, you and I have made Senegal a better place.'

That was it, I could not hold back any longer. I laughed so hard that I started to cry. Pierre gave me this confused look, not quite sure what to make of this scene.

'Are you mocking me, my friend?' he asked. 'Why are you crying?'

'These are tears of joy,' I said, which was not entirely untrue. 'Let's get this show going, let's answer the call of duty.'

'Okay, my friend.' Pierre still did not seem fully convinced that I was not being facetious. 'Give me a few minutes. I will talk to my buddy and be back shortly.'

Pierre left the cell. This time he did not lock the door, probably assuming – correctly – that I would not be willing to flush four hundred dollars down the toilet by disappearing.

Twenty minutes later, Pierre returned with his big, warm smile.

'Good news, my friend,' he said. 'It has all been sorted out. My buddy will fly you to Banjul. The flight leaves in fifteen minutes. Since I don't think you can expect much of an on-board service, I brought you a bottle of water for the flight. Hahaha!'

Pierre wrapped me in a bear hug. 'It was a pleasure spending time with you. Remember your friend Pierre in Dakar and, who knows, maybe one day we'll meet again.'

'The pleasure was all mine,' I said. 'I can assure you that I will not forget this day, and I will never forget you, Pierre.'

As we left the cell, I turned around to get one good look of the place in which I had spent these past surreal hours. The cell seemed a lot less threatening now, just an ordinary room. Funny, how being free changes one's perspective.

Pierre walked me to the gate that led to the tarmac. He reached into his pocket and handed me my passport.

'I think you will need this. Don't try to enter two countries in one day without the necessary documentation,' Pierre said with a chuckle.

I laughed, too. I had totally forgotten about my passport, after all that had happened that day. We hugged one more time, and Pierre unlocked the gate.

After a few steps, I heard Pierre shout 'Stop!' My heart sank instantly. I turned around and saw Pierre signalling for me to come back.

'What's wrong?' I asked.

'Nothing, my friend. But I can't let you board a flight without a boarding pass. That would be just plain wrong.'

'Are you serious?' I asked, convinced Pierre was having some fun at my expense.

'Dead serious,' said Pierre. 'Where would we be if passengers could board flights without boarding passes? Everything needs to have its proper order. The law is the law, and rules are rules. Wait a moment, please.'

Pierre reached behind the counter at the gate and pulled a blank Air Senegal boarding pass out of the drawer. With his pen he wrote 1B in the seat box.

'Why not 1A?' I asked, barely managing to suppress the next bout of laughter.

'Because 1A is reserved for the pilot,' Pierre said with a solemn expression. 'Good luck, my friend, have a safe flight.'

'Thank you, Pierre. Thank you for everything you have done.'

I walked towards the Cessna, where the pilot was awaiting me. He greeted me with a slight nod.

'Have you ever been in one of these?' he asked.

'Actually, yes. I learned to fly on a 152. Though the one I used to fly had doors.'

'Well, it's the same without doors,' he said. 'Climb in. I'll store your briefcase and suitcase behind my seat.'

The inside of the plane was messy, and behind my seat there were a few letters and small boxes, apparently to be delivered in the Gambia. It was a postal plane, after all. My seat was in bad shape, the fabric was dirty and torn. And of course, there were no doors on the sides of the plane, just loose nettings. I wondered whether I had made the mistake of my life getting on this plane – possibly the *last* mistake of my life.

The pilot started the engine immediately and handed me my headset with a mike.

'You'll need this,' he said. 'It gets pretty loud up there, especially with the open sides. You will hear my conversation with the tower, and we can talk to each other during the flight. After takeoff here in Dakar, I don't plan to stay in touch with air traffic control until we are in the final approach to Banjul.'

'Why not?' I asked, by now fully convinced that it had indeed been a bad mistake to board this flight.

'Because these guys are complete morons. The best way to crash a plane in Africa is by paying attention to air traffic control. No sir, we will fly low, about twenty-five hundred feet above ground, all the way to Banjul. It's less than two hundred kilometres, so we will be there in no time. Don't worry.'

'What if air traffic control tries to reach you?' I asked.

'Who gives a crap!' he said, as the plane started to move towards the runway. 'The last time I listened to these pricks, I almost got myself killed. They instructed me to land on a runway at the same time as a 727 was taking off exactly in my direction. No, sir. When I give a damn about what these idiots have to say, I'll be sure to let them know. But that won't be today. Now let's get this baby in the air.'

We took off smoothly, and the flight was beautiful. At some point the pilot asked me whether I wanted to fly the plane, and I took over for about fifteen minutes. Here I was, piloting a doorless Cessna 152 in the African skies. It was surreal.

The pilot got in touch with the tower in Banjul shortly before landing. He seemed on familiar terms with the person in charge, and the landing was smooth. At the end of the runway an old white Land Rover was waiting for me. We stopped the plane, and the driver walked up to my side.

'Mr Levin?'

'Yes, that's me,' I replied.

'Welcome to the Gambia,' he said. 'I've been waiting for you all day, sir. You were supposed to arrive with the Air Afrique flight from Dakar. What happened?'

'It's a long story,' I answered. 'As you can see, I changed my flight to Air Senegal,' I added with a smile.

I said goodbye to the pilot and climbed out of the plane. He handed me my briefcase and my suitcase.

'Good luck,' he said. 'It was nice flying with you. Thank you for the hundred dollars.'

Good old Pierre!

As the plane taxied to the main terminal building to deliver the mail, I got into the Land Rover.

'My name is Amat,' the driver said. 'I am President Jammeh's chief of protocol, and I will be responsible for you during your stay. Let's go. We are already very late.'

*

My meetings in the Gambia turned out to be as unproductive as I had expected, and twenty-two hours after I had landed in Banjul in a single-propeller, open-door plane, I left on a boring, commercial flight to Brussels via Conakry. For a moment I considered travelling back through Dakar in order to say hello to my friend Pierre, but decided to leave that trip for another day, when I could visit with some gifts and a pristine visa in my passport.

PART TWO

Chess à la Russe

'I have asked a good friend of mine to join us for dinner, if you don't mind,' Vitaly said.

'Of course not,' I replied. 'Who is it?'

'I'll explain later,' Vitaly said with a smile. 'Try to keep an open mind. You won't be disappointed.'

I had arrived in Moscow a day earlier for a meeting that Vitaly had arranged with the President of the Russian State Social University to discuss a seminar on financial education. The meeting had been interesting, and Vitaly invited me for dinner at Petrovich, my favourite restaurant in Moscow, so that we could discuss the next steps with the university. Petrovich was a members-only club in a basement of a nondescript building, and decorated in a style reminiscent of Soviet times. I was enjoying my herring with beets – Vitaly called the dish 'herring in a coat' – and a glass of kvass, the fermented drink made from black rye bread. Vitaly and I had become good friends, and he was always generous in introducing me to his contacts, which often reached into the upper echelons of power in Russia.

'Ah, here's Slava,' Vitaly said with a nod towards the hallway.

A handsome man with striking features came to our table, high cheekbones and a powerful chin. He mumbled something to Vitaly and then looked at me.

'Vitaly has given me a thorough briefing on you,' Slava said, as he shook my hand with a firm grip.

I looked at Vitaly with surprise, but he just smiled at me.

'I wish I could say the same thing about you,' I said, throwing Vitaly under the bus, 'but unfortunately our friend here has not told me anything about you, Slava. What do you do?'

'Good old Vitaly,' Slava laughed, 'trying to keep things interesting. Well, Daniel, I am a member of the Duma – you know, that fake parliament we have here in Russia. A fairly well-known member, I might add. But that would be immodest.'

I could hear Vitaly chuckle. These two men were clearly very familiar with each other. There was an air of unspoken mutual understanding between them. Slava waved to the waitress, who immediately came to our table.

'Bring me the usual, please,' Slava told her. 'I have no idea why my new friend here is drinking this Russian horse piss,' he added, pointing at the glass of kvass that I was holding. 'It does taste like horse piss, doesn't it?'

'I wouldn't know,' I said, a little irritated. 'I have never tasted horse piss.'

'Oh, your friend has a sense of humour,' Slava said, looking at Vitaly. 'Feisty. I like that! Daniel, you will need some vodka to disinfect your throat after drinking that!'

'It's not that bad,' I objected meekly.

'It's not that good, either,' Slava replied with a laugh. 'Don't worry, even if your drinking taste leaves something to be desired, you do get high marks for effort and enthusiasm.'

'That's very kind of you,' I said. Slava's patronizing tone was starting to get on my nerves.

Vitaly must have noticed. 'Don't mind Slava,' he said to me with a smile, 'he reserves his most vicious humour for those he likes the most. Evidently, he likes you a lot.'

Slava laughed. He was about to say something when the waitress arrived with a tall glass of water.

'Just water?' I asked. 'After your kvass diatribe, I was expecting something less pedestrian.'

'It's vodka, my friend,' Slava said. 'Good, pure vodka, made of patriotic Russian potatoes. Though in a certain sense you are not wrong – the word "vodka" does come from *voda*, water. Think of it as the diminutive form of *voda*, so, essentially, "little water".'

Slava downed over half his glass in one gulp, and placed it back on the table without any change in his expression. I was sure that he and Vitaly were playing a practical joke on me, and that Slava's glass only contained water.

'Do you mind if I taste your vodka?' I asked Slava.

'Of course, feel free,' he replied with a smile. 'This is a Soviet establishment, so think of us as comrades, on the way to becoming brothers. Happy to share.'

As soon as I put his glass near my face, I could smell the alcohol. Slava read my mind.

'You didn't believe me, did you?' he laughed. 'Remind me to play poker with you. I will be able to retire early.'

'Okay, okay, I confess, I did have my doubts,' I said. 'Can we please start over?'

'Of course,' Slava said. 'Pleased to meet you, Daniel.'

It was evident that Slava's mind and wit were razor-sharp, and I concluded that I would have to work hard just to keep up with him and Vitaly.

This time, it was Vitaly's turn to read my mind.

'Don't worry, Daniel,' he said in a gentle tone, 'Slava makes us all feel dumber than we are. It's a special talent he has, a gift. It's why he is so popular, and why he has been so successful in politics. Oh, wait, he hasn't . . .'

Slava laughed. 'Vitaly likes to rib me because of my opposition to the President and his thugs. He calls me Slava Sisyphusovich. Vitaly thinks my struggle is futile and, therefore, an act of vanity. What do you think?'

'Well, I'm not sure I am in a position to . . .' I started to answer.

'Oh, come on, Daniel,' Slava cut me off. 'We're having dinner at Petrovich, beautiful waitresses, great vodka, excellent food, so no wishy-washiness allowed. Do you think it is futile to take on a battle that seems futile?'

'Is it futile to fight a futile battle? That's like using the defined term in the definition,' I said, feeling suddenly emboldened. 'A big no-no for great thinkers, wouldn't you say?'

'I love this guy!' Slava shouted, looking at Vitaly. 'Where did you find him?'

'He found me,' Vitaly said. 'Anyhow, you answered your own question. Of course your struggle is futile. Noble, perhaps. Principled, perhaps. But still futile. No social purpose, only a personal one. Hence, narcissistic.'

'I know that Vitaly is right,' Slava said, suddenly serious. 'I know that my fight is futile. But it is not an act of vanity. It is the way I am hard-wired. I have no choice but to oppose this regime.'

'God gave you free will, Slava,' Vitaly said. 'Of course you have a choice.'

'Spare me, Vitaly,' Slava said sharply. 'This Russia. The god we have here certainly does not believe in our free will.'

I felt like a spectator at a heavyweight fight.

'If I may ask,' I interjected, 'what is your political platform? What is the basis for your opposition to the President?'

'It's really quite simple, Daniel,' Slava said. 'The President has made any real political debate in Russia impossible. He thinks that protesters and political opponents like myself are against the state, but he's completely wrong. We are *for* a state, but a competent state, a state that takes care of its citizens. It's the President we are against, not the state.'

Slava emptied his glass and ordered another. Vitaly signalled that he wanted one, too.

'You see, Daniel,' Vitaly said, 'our friend Slava here could do so much from the inside. He is on good terms with some key people around the President, and in fact he is very friendly with one of the President's most trusted economic advisers.'

'Ah, yes, Anatoly,' Slava mumbled. 'He studied with my wife. I know him well. A sharp kid.'

'Many of these guys trust and respect Slava,' Vitaly continued. 'He could easily work on an economic programme that benefits the less advantaged. He could do so much. Instead, he fancies himself as a populist tribune, calling out the misdeeds of the powerful. Even if my narcissism comment was a little harsh, he is certainly sacrificing the good and the feasible for the sake of perfection. Which, when it comes to politics, is the mother of all sins.'

'You might be right, Vitaly,' Slava said with a sad expression. 'But it breaks my heart that the President and his cohorts are destroying Russia, Mother Russia, in order to rebuild the Soviet Union. Mark my words: one day, his voracious appetite for power will take him outside Russia's borders, and he will start to gobble up territories in neighbouring countries. Countries that became independent and free when the Soviet Union collapsed.'

'I don't see that happening anytime soon,' I said softly. 'It could lead to war. NATO has been expanding in Russia's direction, and . . .'

'What do you think of that, Daniel?' Slava interrupted me sharply. 'Was it smart to push NATO to Russia's borders? Rest assured that in this country this has turned any possible allies of the United States into sworn enemies. I have to say, America is so incredibly gullible. The mere fact that Madame Albright was born in Prague does not mean that she is an expert on Eastern Europe. Clinton should not have listened to her, he's too clever for that. All that "bigger is better" nonsense that she was whispering into his ear when it came to NATO – I mean, come on now, remind me, please: when has this delightful lady been right on anything? Rwanda? Hong Kong? It seems that this Madame is not all that bright. Hahaha! So tell me, with the benefit of hindsight, do you think it was smart of the Americans to push for this NATO expansion?'

'No, I don't,' I replied after a pause. 'I think it was a mistake. It may end up having tragic consequences, because it will remain a constant reminder of defeat for Russia. A gratuitous humiliation without any upside. After all, let's face it, if Russia ever invaded a former Soviet state such as Latvia or Georgia, it's hard to imagine that the US would send troops to those states to defend them just because they are part of NATO, or have some sort of defence pact with NATO. Their only strategic importance to the US consists in their strategic importance to Russia. So it's a blustery, expensive, empty promise.'

Slava was quiet for a moment, waiting for the waitress to serve the vodka refills. He took a big sip.

'I agree with you,' Slava said. 'I don't think our President will do anything today or tomorrow. But don't be surprised if one day in the future, years from now, he will send in troops to invade a country. He might even annex part of it and claim that it had been Russian all along, and that he was being greeted as a liberator by all the ethnic Russians who live in that territory. And when that happens, trust me, he will be hugely popular at home. A man among boys.'

The waitress arrived with our main courses, and a glass of vodka for me, which Vitaly had surreptitiously ordered.

'Anyhow, enough politics for now,' Slava said. 'It will give us indigestion. I will oppose this President until he decides to serve the people. All the people, that is, not just *his* people. But that is not likely to happen, so I am facing a lonely life in the opposition, with all the consequences that entails. Bon appétit!'

The rest of the evening was lighthearted and pleasant. There was an excellent Russian jazz band that played Miles Davis tunes, and several people stopped by our table to chat with Slava. When we got up to leave, Slava asked me where I was staying.

'At the Metropol Hotel,' I replied.

'Ah, the Metropol,' Slava said. 'Beautiful Art Nouveau, built before the Russian Revolution. Did you know that this is where the KGB henchmen used to meet their girlfriends over lunch for some carnal pleasure?'

'I did not,' I said.

'I hate that place,' Slava said. 'Bad memories.'

'A girlfriend?' Vitaly asked with a chuckle.

Slava winked at Vitaly. Clearly, these two went way back together.

'If you are free, Daniel, why don't I join you for breakfast tomorrow morning, if you pardon my self-invitation,' Slava said. 'I will see if my friend Anatoly is free and bring him along, too, if you don't mind. He really has the President's ear, and you will enjoy meeting him. A very clever fellow. Young, with a bright future. Maybe our busy pal Vitaly can join us, too.'

'That would be lovely,' I said.

The next morning Slava and Anatoly arrived together. As they walked through the lobby the hotel staff treated them both like movie stars. I had done my homework on Anatoly and knew that he was a high-ranking official, but was still taken aback by such a remarkable display of reverence. I assumed that Slava was the incidental beneficiary of Anatoly's VIP status.

The breakfast itself was uneventful. Slava did most of the talking, as gregarious and charming as he had been the previous evening, while Anatoly listened and spoke little. Slava conveyed Vitaly's apologies – apparently, he was at a meeting in the Kremlin. From the way Anatoly looked at Slava, I got the distinct impression that this information was not supposed to be shared with me.

Towards the end of our breakfast, Slava asked me whether I had heard of a certain geopolitical conference that was scheduled to take place in Paris the following week.

'I have indeed,' I answered, a little surprised at the non sequitur. 'As a matter of fact, I was asked to speak at that very conference. Why do you ask?'

'I was asked to attend myself,' Slava said, 'but I may not be able to make it.'

'Probably some very important debates on the floor of the Duma,' Anatoly muttered sarcastically.

'Something like that,' Slava said, clearly not pleased about being on the receiving end of a biting comment from Anatoly.

'Actually, Daniel, I will be in the South of France for a couple of days next week,' Anatoly said, turning to me. 'Is there any chance you could make your way there so that we can talk in peace and quiet? I don't mean to inconvenience you, but since you will already be in Paris, perhaps a little detour to the Côte d'Azur would not be too far out of your way? After all, if you are like me, you will welcome any excuse to spend a day on the French Riviera,' he added with a quiet smile.

I was surprised by Anatoly's question. Up until that point he had not shown much interest in me, and I was wondering why he had agreed to join Slava for breakfast. And now he was asking me to travel from Paris to the South of France just in order to have a quiet conversation. It was a little strange, but at the same time I was intrigued.

'Where exactly will you be?' I asked Anatoly.

'In Cap Ferrat,' he replied.

'I suppose I could come and postpone my trip back to the US by a day or two.'

'That would be nice,' Anatoly said. 'Let's meet on Wednesday morning, if that works for you. Try to stay at La Voile d'Or. It's a lovely hotel, and we could meet for breakfast on the terrace. It's a very pleasant place to talk.'

'Why not, that sounds nice.'

Anatoly got up and told me that he had to run to a meeting.

'See you next Wednesday for breakfast. Let's make it nine o'clock,' he said as he shook my hand.

'Nine sounds fine, I'm looking forward to it.'

Slava walked Anatoly to the entrance of the restaurant, and then came back to the table.

'Well, what's your impression of Anatoly?' he asked me.

'Hard to tell, he did not say very much,' I replied. 'What did he think of me?'

'Oh, he definitely liked you. Otherwise he would not have asked you to meet him in France next week.'

'Yeah, I was a little surprised by that,' I said. 'Do you know what he wants to talk about?'

'Well, as you know, he and I are on opposite sides of the political game, I mean political spectrum, so I am not privy to his secrets. But if I had to take an educated guess, I would say that he wants to discuss some political or economic initiative with you. Remember, he reports to the Godfather, the *capo di tutti capi*.'

'You know, Slava, it felt to me like you and Anatoly were close. It must be awkward for the two of you to be friends, given how vocal you have been in your opposition to the President.'

'Don't forget, my friend, this is Russia,' Slava said with a laugh. 'Things aren't always obvious and linear here.'

Slava informed me that he and his wife would be in the US the following month, and we agreed to touch base a few days before his arrival, so that we could arrange when and where to meet. On a whim, I offered that he could stay in our home if he found himself in the New York area, and, to my surprise, Slava immediately accepted my invitation. We parted on a cordial note.

That evening I went for a walk with Vitaly on the beautifully lit Red Square. The Kremlin's walls, the Lenin Mausoleum, the unusual colours of St Basil's Cathedral and its onion domes, they all left me with the exhilarating feeling of being close to power. I was grateful to Vitaly for his introduction to Slava and, through Slava, to Anatoly, and I told him about the breakfast conversation and Anatoly's invitation to meet him in Cap Ferrat.

'I really appreciate your generosity in introducing me to your friends, Vitaly,' I said as we strolled over the uneven cobblestones.

'Don't thank me too soon,' Vitaly answered. 'You have to be alert around these guys. They are very clever and very driven. They are charming and entertaining in their intellect, but don't be fooled by the intimacy. If it serves their needs, they will eat you and spit you out. And you won't even notice.'

'Come on, Vitaly,' I laughed. 'I think you have been in Russia too long, you have become paranoid. They both seem to be decent fellows.'

'Don't ever say someone is a decent person, until you have seen him be tested,' Slava shot back with a serious look. 'Enjoy their company, and relish their proximity to power. But don't ever fall into the trap of believing that they are your friends. Don't forget, we are in Moscow. There are no friends here.'

'Wow, you sure have a way of putting a damper on a man's good mood,' I said, putting my hand on Vitaly's shoulder. 'I'm starving, let's go somewhere nice and have dinner.'

Vitaly's wife and daughter joined us for dinner at a restaurant near their home. The evening was very pleasant, and I was sad that I had to leave Moscow the next morning. After dinner, Vitaly drove me back to the hotel. He gave me a big hug when we parted.

'Please remember, Daniel,' Vitaly said with an earnest expression, 'Anatoly is an outstanding chess player.'

'I'll keep that in mind. But not to worry, I have no intention of challenging him to a game of chess,' I said lightheartedly.

'I don't think you understand, Daniel. For these guys, life is a game of chess,' Vitaly said. 'Anatoly does not plan one or two moves in advance. He plans twenty or thirty moves ahead, as many as it takes. The only question is where exactly you fit into their endgame plans.'

'With all due respect, I don't think I play any role in Anatoly's endgame plans,' I said laughingly, 'though it is flattering to consider that I might.'

'Be careful what you wish for,' Vitaly whispered. 'Trust me, if he or his boss had no interest in you, he would not have asked you to come to Cap Ferrat. Take care.'

I was sure that Vitaly was exaggerating the Machiavellian mystique of Kremlin power brokers, and I did not give his Cassandra warnings much thought.

I arrived in Cap Ferrat the following Tuesday evening and checked into the lovely La Voile d'Or hotel. At check-in I asked the receptionist whether Anatoly had already arrived. I was a little taken aback when she informed me that she had no reservation under his name, and for a moment I wondered whether Anatoly was playing a cruel joke on me. But I told myself that he probably refrained from announcing his travel schedule to the world, and that his reservation might have been made under a different name. I went for a long walk past the harbour along the waterfront, and then had dinner by myself on the lovely terrace of the hotel. Still, I went to sleep that night with some doubt whether Anatoly would actually show up.

At exactly nine o'clock the next morning a limousine with tinted windows pulled up to the hotel entrance, and – to my great relief – out stepped Anatoly. He motioned to his bodyguards to stay in the car, rather than follow him into the hotel.

'Very nice to see you again, Anatoly,' I said as we shook hands. 'For a moment, you had me worried that you would not show up.'

'Why is that?' Anatoly asked, seeming genuinely surprised.

'Because the hotel had no reservation under your name, and I did not see you last night or this morning.'

'That's because I am not staying here,' Anatoly said matter-of-factly.

'Well, I thought, since you had suggested that I stay here . . .'

'I thought you would like it,' Anatoly explained, 'and the terrace is lovely for breakfast. But our delegation is staying at the Grand-Hôtel. Anyhow, shall we?'

We sat down at our table and ordered something to drink. Coffee for me, tea for Anatoly. We chatted for a few minutes about our families, and I decided to get to the point.

'Please forgive the direct question,' I said, 'but I am curious why you proposed that we meet.'

'Fair enough,' he said. 'Slava had told me about your financial literacy work, and he mentioned this platform you have, focused on education and capacity building. It seemed important to my boss that we learn more about it.'

'Why?' I asked.

'Let me put it to you this way,' Anatoly continued. 'Just recently, the President told me that in his estimate there are no more than one thousand five hundred people in Moscow and St Petersburg together with the requisite skills to function in the financial markets. Please note that I said "function", not "thrive". This includes regulators, legislators, judges, bankers, lawyers, and so on. Just fifteen hundred. Imagine that!'

'That's hard to believe,' I said. 'This number seems incredibly low. Fifteen hundred – that's an average office building on Wall Street! And you are saying that this is all there is in Moscow?'

'Moscow *and* St Petersburg,' Anatoly replied. 'And I am not the one saying it; the President is. So it is the gospel.'

Anatoly's face did not reveal any emotion, so I was not sure whether his last comment was meant sarcastically.

'In any event,' he continued, 'the President thought your platform might be an excellent platform, pardon the pun, to multiply the knowledge base as quickly as possible through its teach-the-teacher methodology. If we cannot accomplish this, we might be facing a calamity in our financial sector. Already, we are witnessing an epidemic of pyramid schemes. People are losing their life savings, the little they have.'

'What about the rest of the country?' I asked.

'Moscow and St Petersburg *are* the country,' Anatoly replied, 'at least as far as finance and culture are concerned.'

'I see.'

'So when Slava told me about you,' Anatoly continued, 'I mentioned this to the President, and he asked me to feel you out, so to speak. He also asked me to arrange for a meeting between you and Andrei Kozlov. Have you ever met him?'

'I'm afraid I haven't.'

'Kozlov is the First Deputy Chairman of our Central Bank. He is a brilliant man, and also a personal friend. I consider Kozlov to be the cleanest man in Russia, completely incorruptible. He is the father of deposit insurance in the Russian banking system. He made himself quite a few enemies by revoking the licences of banks suspected of money laundering or other criminal activities. Some of his enemies are powerful, and I must confess that I worry about his safety.'

'I would be delighted to meet him,' I said.

'Good,' Anatoly said. 'Should I just put you in touch with his office, or would you prefer if I go through Vitaly or Slava, who also know Kozlov?'

'I would be happy to connect directly with his office,' I replied. 'There's no need to inconvenience Vitaly or Slava. Actually, I have a question about Slava, if you don't mind.'

'Sure, what is it?'

'I understand that Slava is opposed to your President,' I said, 'and I myself have heard him utter some pretty aggressive things about how the new ruling class is destroying Russia. How is it that you and Slava can allow yourselves to be on such good terms? After all, you work closely with the President.'

Anatoly smiled and was quiet for a moment.

'Do you play chess, Daniel?' he finally asked.

'A little,' I replied.

'Then let me rephrase,' he said, deliberately enunciating each word. 'How well do you play chess?'

'Not very well by *your* standards, I suppose.'

'I will answer your question with a chess analogy, if you don't mind,' Anatoly said. 'Most people think that the most brilliant tactical move in chess is the pawn sacrifice. But it isn't. In fact, it is rather ordinary. There are many sacrifices in chess – deflection sacrifices, positional sacrifices, and the like. The only piece you cannot sacrifice is the king. Are you following me?'

'Yes, I think I am.'

'Then your chess is not too bad,' Anatoly said with a smile. 'Anyhow, the move that really does require tactical genius is castling. Think about it: it is the only move in chess that allows you to move two pieces simultaneously. It provides defence for the king and offence for the rook at the same time. But what I really love about castling is that even though you do it early in the game, it is the endgame that you have in mind. This is what separates the beginners from the masters, the boys from the men. The ability to think ahead, to position yourself for the long run.'

Anatoly had worked himself into a mini-ecstasy during his castling homily. He instantly seemed to regret this uncharacteristic display of passion, and retreated into his sombre shell.

'Castling is the best way I can answer your question about Slava,' he continued after a pause. 'In Russia, relationships are not always what they seem to be on first blush. If Slava survives his pubescent, rebellious phase, he might resurface one day in a very different, unexpected role. Who knows.'

I tried to digest what Anatoly had just told me, but was struggling to make sense of it. Anatoly seemed to insinuate that there was more to the hostility between Slava and the President than what met the eye, and that perhaps Slava's demonstrative opposition was just an act. I decided to ask the question directly.

'Please forgive me if my question is indiscreet, but . . .'

'There are no indiscreet questions, just indiscreet answers,' Anatoly interrupted me.

'Funny, my grandmother used to say the very same thing,' I said. 'Anyway, if you don't mind the question, I wonder whether Slava just serves a token opposition role for the Kremlin, whether the President controls Slava, so to speak.'

Anatoly smiled and did not reply immediately.

'I'll answer your question indirectly,' he finally said. 'It is the only way I can.'

'Of course, I understand.'

'Do you know what Pascal's Wager is?' Anatoly asked.

'Yes, I believe I do.'

'How would you describe it?' he insisted. 'What is your understanding of Pascal's Wager?'

'Well,' I said, a little irritated at being quizzed like a high-schooler, 'if I am not mistaken, it is essentially the rational answer to the question of whether God exists. Pascal argued that if we are faced with the choice of believing that God exists versus believing that he does not exist, then the only sensible decision is to bet on God's existence.'

'Exactly,' Anatoly said with a smirk. 'And why is it the only rational bet for us?'

'Because if we bet on God's existence and we are wrong, there's no real downside,' I replied, feeling like a proud schoolboy who had just given the correct answer, and now has a chance to go for extra credit. 'But if we bet on God's non-existence and we are wrong, then we are really screwed,' I continued. 'So the only rational choice is to assume that God exists and is omnipotent.'

'Indeed,' Anatoly said. 'And that is precisely how it is with our President, whether it relates to Slava or anyone else, present company included.'

I felt like I was talking to an oracle. Throughout our conversation Anatoly had been several steps ahead of me, and I needed some time to gather my thoughts and catch up. I tried to steer the conversation away from the President and Slava, and we spent the next thirty minutes discussing our financial education platform and how it could be implemented in Russia. I was in the midst of describing the platform's main features, when Anatoly's phone rang. He looked at the number on the display and stood up even before answering the call. After saying '*da*' three times, Anatoly ended the call and informed me that he had to leave immediately. I walked him to his limousine, where the bodyguards were waiting. Without another word he disappeared behind the tinted windows, and the car drove off.

I went for a long walk to clear my thoughts. I felt completely outclassed by Anatoly's analytical brilliance, but I was also hugely intrigued by the riddles and the mystery of it all. Slava's visit in the US would feel like a continuation of this conversation with Anatoly. I was looking forward to it.

A few weeks after meeting Anatoly in Cap Ferrat, Slava sent me an email confirming his travel plans. He informed me that his wife Olga would be accompanying him, and asked whether the invitation to our home was still valid. I replied that indeed it was, and that my family looked forward to hosting him and Olga. Slava asked me to join him in Washington for a meeting with several members of Congress who had expressed an interest in Russia, and we agreed to travel back to New York together after that meeting.

Slava and I met in Washington four days later. He and Olga were staying at the Willard near the White House. Judging by the familiarity with which the hotel staff were treating him, he seemed to be a regular guest. We walked together up Pennsylvania Avenue to Capitol Hill. Passing some homeless people leaning against a building, Slava remarked how pleased he was that not all the homeless people on this planet lived in Russia.

The meeting with the members of Congress was intended to be a celebration of Slava's courageous opposition to the Russian President. He was basking in the adulation, but when he was asked about his opinion on America's foreign policy, the atmosphere turned a little tense.

'Sometimes, I get the impression that the leadership of this great country of yours is not clear about the objectives of its foreign adventures,' Slava said. 'Are you defending democracy or fighting for freedom? Or are you just shooting for regime change, so to speak? Or, to paraphrase one of your past presidents, are you just trying to replace someone else's son of a bitch with your son of a bitch? Which is it?'

One senator responded that regime change was usually behind these foreign adventures, for better or for worse, but that the US had unfortunately not been very effective in getting it done.

'Well, we Russians had decades of experience with regime change throughout the Soviet Union,' Slava said with a laugh. 'We figured out the best way to install whom we liked in these vassal countries of ours.'

'How did you do it?' the senator asked.

'With trickery, of course,' Slava replied, 'with a hook. You guys are too linear. You always confuse correlation with causation. Maybe your sycophancy for liberty and freedom has ruined you. You think these conflicts are staring contests, and whoever blinks first loses. But that's not how it works. You lack some good old KGB training. Our President may be a nasty piece of work, but he sure ain't stupid. If you want regime change, you set a red line that you know the other side will cross, so that you can take out the leadership because it crossed the red line. Sometimes, you even nudge them across the red line, if you have to. Perhaps with something light and creative, like a few bombings in your own capital, so that you can ride the popular anger all the way to the military intervention. And conversely, if you *don't* want regime change, you set a red line that you know the other side will *not* cross, so that you can justify your non-intervention to your own hawks back home. Easy peasy, as you say. Just your basic power politics.'

The senator and the other attending members of Congress looked completely lost.

'Yeah, yeah, I get it,' the senator finally said. Judging by the vacant look on his face, that was hardly the case.

'The one thing you don't do,' Slava continued, 'is set a red line, and then not act when it is crossed. It makes you look weak, like a wimp. The world is not a place for nuance. The meanest dog usually gets the biggest bone. Or, in our case, the meanest bear,' he added with a laugh.

The members of Congress in the room did not quite know what to make of this meeting. They had showed up with the intention of honouring Slava as a freedom fighter for his public and courageous opposition to the Kremlin. Instead, they found themselves being lectured, even mocked, by this intense Russian. I got the sense that Slava was bored. A debate with this crowd was no challenge to him; it was too easy, like fishing with dynamite. The meeting petered out, and we left shortly afterwards. Olga met us at Union Station with their luggage, and we boarded a train to New York.

We spent a lovely evening together at our home. After dinner, I opened another bottle of wine and Slava and I sat outside on the porch, overlooking the Hudson River. None of us spoke for a while.

'I know that I gave you the impression that I hate our President,' Slava said finally.

'Well, do you?' I asked.

'Sometimes,' he said. 'Just like I hate myself sometimes.'

'What do you mean?'

'It's all a game,' Slava said. 'No matter what anyone tells you, nobody in this game is fighting for ideals, or for Mother Russia.'

'So what is everyone fighting for?' I asked.

'For power,' he replied. 'Raw power, in its ugly glory.'

'Is it worth it?'

Slava paused for a long time. 'That's a good question,' he said. 'A very good question. I cannot answer that. But I do know that Danton was right, that revolutions do indeed devour their own children.'

'If that's how you feel, then why are you still battling the President, paying such a high price?'

'That's an even better question,' Slava said with a forlorn expression. 'Probably because I like the challenge and the attention. And I enjoy the game, much to Olga's chagrin.'

We spent the rest of the evening talking about other things, and at around midnight Slava decided to call it a day.

'Time to join my wife,' he said with a smirk, 'or she will think that I disappeared, yet again. I do have the tendency to do so, you know, from time to time. Nothing personal, just a bad habit, I suppose. Good night.'

'Good night.' I had no idea what he meant, but I assumed the amount of wine we had consumed that evening might have had something to do with his peculiar parting statement.

The next morning Slava and Olga left early. He was scheduled to give a speech at Columbia University, and from there he and Olga would go straight to the airport to catch a flight to Paris.

I walked him to the car that was waiting for him in our driveway, and he gave me a bear hug.

'Goodbye, my friend,' he said. 'It might be a while before we see each other again. As I told you last night, I have a tendency to dis-appear from time to time. But we will meet again one day, and when we do, things might be different.'

Once again I had no idea what Slava was talking about. He was very much a public figure in Russia, a member of the Duma, and a ubiquitous presence on the international lecture circuit, so it was not clear to me why he should suddenly disappear. I attributed his parting words to his Russian penchant for melodrama, and did not give it a second thought.

About three weeks later, I got a call from the assistant of First Deputy Chairman Andrei Kozlov of the Russian Central Bank. She informed me that the First Deputy Chairman had been briefed by Anatoly and requested a meeting with me. We agreed on a date ten days later. I called Vitaly, who was already aware of this meeting.

A few days before I left for Moscow, I sent Slava a message to let him know that I would be in town, but received no reply. After I arrived, I tried to call him, but he did not pick up. I asked Vitaly whether he had seen Slava recently, and he said that he had not.

'Come to think of it,' Vitaly continued, 'it has been a while since I have seen him. I heard that he resigned from the Duma and has left politics, but I have no idea where he is or what he is doing these days.'

The news of Slava's resignation from the Duma caught me by surprise. I remembered his strange prediction of his own disappearing act when he left our home. Maybe he had to go underground for his own safety. I hoped that nothing horrible had happened to him and his family.

The meeting with Kozlov was encouraging. He was well prepared and informed, even beyond what he could have gleaned from Anatoly. Kozlov seemed genuinely interested in a joint financial development project with our firm. He liked our methodology of transferring the know-how to local, Russian professionals, and helping them design and implement the necessary reforms, rather than having outsiders tell Russians what to do.

'We had some horrible experiences with those genius Harvard boys in the early nineties,' Kozolv said with emotion. 'Yeltsin and Chubais and Gaidar basically gave Jeffrey Sachs and his Harvard wonder-kids carte blanche to do as they pleased in Russia. It was an unmitigated disaster. The economic reforms and privatizations not only failed, but actually contributed towards the descent of the economy into a criminal abyss. We have still not recovered. I feel like we have been living in the Wild West ever since.'

'Some of those Harvard wonder-kids are smart guys who have gone on to have highly respected careers,' I said, trying to defuse the situation.

'The problem is not their lack of intelligence or intellect,' Kozlov shot back. 'It's their humungous arrogance.'

Kozlov explained how he and Anatoly considered our approach the exact opposite of the misguided initiatives in the early 1990s. We spent two hours discussing the framework of a joint initiative between the Central Bank and our firm, and parted on a positive note. The ball was in my court to revert to Kozlov with a specific proposal – selecting the participating professionals on the Russian side, timeline, milestones, and budget. I was very taken by Kozlov.

He was a real doer, not just full of empty words. I left Moscow in a buoyant mood.

Two weeks later, I was in my office in New York when I received a call from Vitaly. I could immediately tell from his voice that something was very wrong.

'A terrible thing happened this evening. Andrei Kozlov is dead.'

I was stunned. 'What . . . no . . . how?'

'Two gunmen shot him and his driver at a sports complex in Moscow. He leaves behind a widow and three little children.'

I was unable to speak. The words were stuck in my throat. I felt like someone had hit me over the head with a sledgehammer.

'I thought you would want to know,' Vitaly continued. 'Welcome to today's Russia.'

It took me a long time to recover from Kozlov's assassination. I had taken a great liking to this man and was looking forward to working together with him and his team. He was the kind of person who could help build a better future for Russia, someone who would make Russia proud. And now he was gone, killed for trying to do the right thing. Anatoly had been eerily prescient in his premonition. I could not get Kozlov's wife and children out of my mind. I got the sense that his death greatly affected Vitaly, too, even though he spoke very little of it.

I knew from Vitaly that Slava and Kozlov had been close friends. Over the coming months, I tried to reach Slava a few more times, and sent him two emails. I never received a reply, and at some point I stopped trying. I never heard from Slava again, and eventually I forgot about him.

Eight years later, I was watching the news in a hotel room in London, when my old friend Slava popped up on the television screen. He was giving an interview on the crisis in the Ukraine. But I could make no sense of what he was saying. Instead of criticizing the Kremlin as he had done so aggressively in the past, he was instead praising the Russian President as the liberator of the Ukrainian people. I almost fell off my chair listening to the words coming out of Slava's mouth. He was attacking Europe and the US for their anti-Russian propaganda, for ignoring and undermining the Ukraine's historical and cultural ties to Russia, for mercilessly exploiting the Ukrainian people, even for massacring and raping women and children in Donbass. He called the European Union a fascist organization that had orchestrated a military coup in the Ukraine and installed a puppet government in Kiev, a bunch of mercenaries and whores, operating in the same way as the Nazis had. Slava alleged that Western Europe was completely controlled and dominated by the American secret service. He spoke in a calm and steady voice, claiming that the West's behaviour was tantamount to a declaration of war against Russia, and warned that Western leaders should be careful what they wished for because they were messing with the wrong man, and that Russia stood united behind its President. The West would soon learn how tough the Russian President really was. If war was what the West wanted, then war it would get.

I sat on my hotel bed, staring at the television in complete shock. The man on the screen did look like Slava, but the words coming out of his mouth sounded like those of another person. I wondered whether perhaps some Russian thugs were holding Slava's family at gunpoint, forcing him to utter this propaganda on television. But in the following days I saw and read many more such statements from Slava, each one more vitriolic than the last one. This was not some timid prisoner speaking publicly against his own inner convictions. No, this was a man on a mission, defending his President in the most primal way imaginable.

I was completely flabbergasted. I remembered Slava's stay in our home all those years ago and wondered whether I had been the unwitting host of a Russian one-man sleeper cell.

Two weeks after watching Slava eviscerate the European Union and the US on television, I met Vitaly for dinner in Zurich. He was waiting for me at the entrance of the restaurant with a big smile.

'Good evening, Daniel,' he said in a jovial tone. 'I'm so happy to see you. It has been a while. How are you?'

'I'm fine, thanks,' I replied. 'Actually, not so well.'

'What happened? Nothing serious, I hope.' Vitaly looked genuinely concerned.

'No, no, nothing like that. It's about Slava. I am completely confused. He disappeared for eight years, not to be found. He did not reply to any messages, did not return any calls, even after Kozlov was killed. And now, after eight years, he resurfaces. And boy, does he ever resurface! Now he is the President's number one henchman in the Ukrainian crisis. He went from being the President's enemy to being his hitman! That's a little radical, wouldn't you say?'

Vitaly smiled and grabbed my arm, leading me to our table. We sat down, and he asked the waiter to bring us a bottle of the house Chianti. We sat in silence until the waiter returned with the wine and filled our glasses.

'You seem very upset,' Vitaly started. 'Try not to be. Keep an open mind, and perhaps you will end up seeing things a little differently, when it's all said and done.'

'I'll do my best. But please tell me, Vitaly, what is this about? Is this the same Slava you introduced me to all those years ago? The same Slava who attacked your President whenever and wherever he could?'

'Yes, Daniel,' Vitaly said calmly. 'It's the same Slava.'

'I'm sorry, I am really confused,' I said. 'How can that be? He used to ooze contempt for the Kremlin with every fibre of his soul. He defined his entire political persona as being the anti-President. His battles might have been quixotic, but he was nothing if not principled. I just don't get it.'

Vitaly took a long sip of wine. 'I suppose it is theoretically possible that Slava simply changed his mind about the regime. Or did he? Hmm, what an intriguing conundrum,' he added with a smile.

Vitaly was silent for a moment, looking at his glass of wine. I held my tongue.

'I just love this wine,' he finally continued. 'Anyone who spends a fortune on some fancy French wine is a fool. Give me a carafe of a simple Chianti any day.'

Vitaly's demonstrative display of pleasure over a glass of plain wine was getting on my nerves, but I knew him well enough not to interrupt him.

'Anyhow,' he continued after another sip, 'do you remember the evening at Petrovich, the first time you met Slava?'

'I certainly do. He was so dynamic, so fearless. Everyone there seemed to know and respect him, and he didn't hide his contempt for the President.'

'Exactly,' Vitaly said.

'What do you mean, exactly?' I was confused.

'As you said, he did not hide his contempt. Didn't you ever ask yourself whether Slava was crazy to criticize the Kremlin so publicly?' Vitaly asked.

'Well . . .'

Vitaly cut me off. 'Did you ever wonder why Slava never suffered negative repercussions for his loud and demonstrative opposition?'

'Well . . .'

Again, Vitaly cut me off. 'Think, Daniel. Think. It's not illegal yet. This is Russia we are talking about. People have been locked up for far less than what Slava has been doing. Even some pretty powerful guys, guys who seemed untouchable, until one day they weren't. So why do you think Slava could walk around kicking the President's butt with impunity? Why?'

'I don't know. What are you saying, Vitaly? Are you implying that Slava was the President's man all along?'

Vitaly smiled.

'Seriously?' I asked.

'Tell me, Daniel, how good is your chess?' Vitaly asked.

'Funny, the last person who asked me that question was Anatoly, when we met in Cap Ferrat all those years ago.'

'Well, how good is it?'

'Evidently not good enough,' I replied.

Vitaly laughed. 'Don't be so hard on yourself. Anyway, in chess there is an important move called castling. Are you familiar with it?'

This time, it was my turn to laugh. 'Did you and Anatoly rehearse this? He was also extolling the virtues of castling. What is it with the two of you and castling?'

'I was hoping it would be obvious by now,' Vitaly said, sounding genuinely disappointed in me. 'Castling is a switching move you make early in the game, with the king and the rook, by the way, which makes the whole analogy to our friend Slava even more delicious. But the most important point of castling is that it is a move you make early in the game in order to set yourself up for the endgame. You have to be able to plan twenty moves in advance, and you have to be disciplined to hide your plans until it is time to go for the kill.'

I finally understood. Slava must have been in the President's camp all along, though I was still not sure whether all this had been an incredibly elaborate plot to penetrate and control the political opposition, or whether it was just a case of chaos theory, Kremlin-style. Either way, it explained Slava's close relationship with Anatoly, and it explained the impunity with which he had moved and spoken so freely during his years in the opposition. I was amazed at his self-control and ability to stick to the script. He had remained dormant for more than eight long years, to be activated in time for the President's Ukrainian adventure. It was quite remarkable.

The waiter came to take our orders.

'I have never seen anything like this,' I said to Vitaly as soon as the waiter left. 'I don't know whether to be impressed or terrified. Probably both, I suppose.'

'Well, there is a silver lining, isn't there?' Vitaly said with a sheepish look. Just like with Anatoly, I felt as if I was being continuously tested.

'And what would that be?'

'At least a game of chess follows clear rules,' Vitaly said. 'This is what I keep telling myself. It is the one thing that has kept me from giving up or going crazy.'

'Wow, that's quite the silver lining!' I said.

'I know,' Vitaly continued. 'It's how the dispossessed console themselves as they grasp for straws. Pathetic, perhaps, but remember this: the moment to be really scared is when that changes, when those in power replace chess with a game that has no rules.'

I fell silent. The restaurant suddenly felt much darker.

'Cheer up, Daniel!' Vitaly said with a smile. 'How do you say? We are playing chess, while you are playing checkers?'

'We don't say that,' I corrected him. 'You do!'

Vitaly smiled. 'Exactly.'

Never again did we discuss Slava – or chess for that matter.

Very Foggy Bottom

A few months after my dinner with Vitaly in Zurich, I met my friend Nigel Broadband for tea in one of Manhattan's upscale social clubs. Nigel was an interesting fellow. Very accomplished, Oxford degree, political adviser, journalist for a prestigious British publication, tasteful sartorial choices, great hair with just the right amount of grey, rimless spectacles, impeccable accent – the complete package.

Without naming any names, I told Nigel about the experience with Slava.

'Well, old boy,' Nigel said when I finished my account, 'I'd say that Stephen King was right after all, wasn't he: "Monsters are real, and ghosts are real too. They live inside us, and sometimes, they win." The man knows of what he speaks. Or rather, of what he writes. Scary stuff indeed.'

Nigel summoned the waiter and berated him for serving green tea in boiling hot water.

'This Sencha tea should be brewed and served at seventy degrees Celsius, or, for you Yankees, one hundred and sixty degrees Fahrenheit,' he chided the poor man. 'Good Lord! Talk about casting pearls before swine.'

The waiter took the pot of tea and mumbled something under his breath.

'What was that?' Nigel asked sharply.

'He was probably converting your Celsius guidelines into Kelvin,' I said quickly in an attempt to defuse the unpleasant situation.

Nigel laughed. 'Anyhow, let's leave these Russian monsters and ghosts for a few moments. There is something else I would like to talk to you about.'

'What's that?' I asked.

'Since our last meeting in London, I have been doing some thinking about that development platform of yours. I like it, I really do. I could be your biggest fan.'

'But?'

'But you are wasting a good thing. It's time to graduate to the premier league. It's time for me to take you from where you are today to where you should be tomorrow. From here to there,' he added, moving his left hand from his feet to his head. I suppose that was as high as things could go.

I was flattered by Nigel's enthusiasm for our platform, even if I knew that Nigel was prone to superlatives – evidently not a big believer in British understatement. It was the contrarian in him, which made him even more appealing.

The waiter returned with Nigel's tea and placed it wordlessly on the table with an exaggerated motion.

'Daniel, take my word for it,' Nigel said, completely ignoring the waiter, 'you will do magnificent things. You are marked for greatness. Please do remember to mention me in your Nobel Peace Prize acceptance speech in Oslo.'

I knew it was tongue-in-cheek, but I still enjoyed his hyperbole. 'Come on, Nigel,' I said, 'let's keep it real.'

'Okay, okay, maybe not the Nobel Peace Prize. Maybe one of the smaller ones,' he added, laughing. 'But, all joking aside, I really do believe you have something special here. One would have to be mad not to fall in love with what you are doing. I mean, development by transferring knowledge and complete toolkits to local talent . . . Come on, now! That has never been done before with such an intellectually honest methodology.'

'Enough, Nigel,' I said, a little uncomfortable. It would have been easier to take his compliments seriously if he had tempered his enthusiasm.

'No, Daniel, it has to be said,' Nigel continued. 'What you need is to hook up with a major public player. Not those clowns at the World Bank or the IMF, and not those useless development agencies such as DFID or USAID. No, you should go straight to the heavyweight. The thousand-pound gorilla.'

'You mean the eight-hundred-pound gorilla?' I corrected him.

'My point exactly, Daniel. Stop thinking small. The only one who can kick the eight-hundred-pound gorilla's arse is the thousand-pound gorilla. No, sir, what you need is the State Department.'

'The State Department?' I had not seen that one coming.

'Indeed, old boy. The State Department is the one that can take you from where you are now all the way to the top of the world. They have what you need, and you have what they need. They have the global stage and the authority of the sole remaining super-power, with apologies to my beloved yet decrepit Britain. And you have the content, the substance that they so obviously lack. It's a marriage made in heaven.'

'It is an interesting thought,' I said, increasingly intrigued. 'Though I thought this would seem to be more up Treasury's alley. I've worked with Treasury on African initiatives before; they used to have an excellent person heading their Africa desk. State, on the other hand, is a rather tedious outfit to work with.'

'You speaketh the truth,' Nigel said with a chuckle. 'Under normal circumstances, I would have to be out of my mind, or really cruel, to recommend the State Department to a friend. But I have a contact there who might be just what the doctor ordered.'

'And why's that?' I asked.

'This fellow works within a division, or a group or task force – I don't know exactly how it is denominated, but who cares? – that has the mandate to connect with the private sector and work together on all sorts of interesting initiatives. In essence, it's State's attempt at institutionalizing private-public partnerships.'

'Yes, I'm aware of it,' I said. 'It's headed by a former congressional staffer of the Secretary. But from what I've heard, it's not very effective.'

'Precisely,' Nigel said. 'It's not effective at all. But not for lack of effort, not for lack of networking, and not for lack of interest by the private sector. The reason this task force has been irrelevant is that it has no substantive platform whatsoever, no real calling, if you get my drift. When companies like Microsoft or Procter & Gamble or Exxon or Boeing or Citibank contact the State Department to do something together in a target market, and these heavyweights are willing to back it up with serious money, State has nothing substantive to offer. Nothing. And that is where you guys come in.'

'It sounds interesting,' I said. 'But how would the cooperation with us work? How would we be integrated?'

'Come on now, Daniel,' Nigel explained, 'don't act more densely than you already are. Do I have to chew it for you, too? Show some imagination! Let's say Coca-Cola concludes that there's a region in Ethiopia where not enough people consume Coke, heaven forbid. Now, it would be in bad taste – if you can indulge the unforgivably bland pun – for them to go to the Ethiopian government and give them hell, wouldn't it? Let's say they try for a subtler, gentler approach. Let's say Coca-Cola approaches the State Department and says: "Look, guys, we need to sell more Coke in Ethiopia, and you need better relations and more influence in the Horn of Africa. How about we sponsor one of your fancy diaspora initiatives? There are about a gazillion and a half Ethiopians living in DC and its suburbs alone, of which half a gazillion seem to be taxi drivers. Let's mobilize them and try to get them to go back to their home country and build capacity on the ground. Reverse the brain drain, so to speak." So far, so good?'

'So far, so good,' I answered. 'But still, how do we fit in?'

'Let me spell it out for you,' Nigel said, sounding deliberately exasperated. 'State loves the idea, because it gets its bills paid by Coca-Cola. Coca-Cola loves the idea because it gets to hide its self-serving commercial interests – let's create more sugar addicts and diabetics in Africa – behind the US government's feel-good, hot-air diaspora initiative. But there's one minor problem . . .'

'Which is?'

'Which is that neither the State Department nor Coca-Cola have a clue how to implement this initiative in Ethiopia. No idea how to build capacity, how to generate financial inclusion, vocational training, how to transfer know-how. So all this fancy speak of a diaspora initiative is nothing but a hollow platitude, like pretty much everything emanating from the State Department. They need the content provider, someone to design and implement the substance of the initiative. Someone with a ready-to-market platform. They need you. Q.E.D., old boy. Q.E.D.'

Nigel had made a compelling case, and I really wanted to believe him. But over the years I had suffered through so many discouraging and frustrating experiences with the State Department, irrespective of the particular Secretary of State or the political party in power. I wasn't up for another colossal waste of time, DC-style.

'I like what you're proposing, Nigel, I really do,' I said.

'But?' Nigel interrupted.

'But my past interactions with State have been somewhat dispiriting, to put it mildly,' I continued. 'The State Department is a very strange place. A place full of self-importance and hot air, as you so aptly put it, with very little tangible output.'

'*À qui le dis-tu?*' Nigel said. 'Believe me, I know. They are a bunch of wankers! But I think this time, it could work out. In any case, why not give it a try? The guy I know there is Nate Kleiner. Little Nate, as I call him, much to his chagrin. A real DC lifer, has been bouncing around between government agencies and development institutions. Bit of a tool, I'm afraid, but harmless. If you don't mind, I'll give him a call and tell him about you. I'll let him contact you. How does that sound?'

'Sure, why not?' I replied. 'If it works out, I owe you a drink. If not, and I will end up wasting my time as expected, you'll buy me a drink. A few drinks, actually. Some really old Macallan.'

Nigel laughed. 'It's a deal. Either way, we'll have some good whisky. Sounds like a win-win to me.'

The next day my phone rang. The caller had a Virginia area code.

'Hi, this is Nathan.'

I had an inkling that this might be Nigel's contact, but hesitated for a moment.

'Nathan. Nathan Kleiner. Nate. Nigel Broadband's friend.'

'Oh, Nate, I'm so sorry,' I said. 'It took me a moment to put it together. I wasn't expecting your call so soon.'

'Well, Nigel called me yesterday and told me about you, and that I should make sure not to die without having met you,' Nate said.

'That sounds like Nigel, alright,' I said, 'raising expectations to the point where I can only disappoint.'

Nate laughed. 'No worries, I'll apply the Nigel-discount factor. I'm sure he also praised me to you in superlatives. Anyway, I will be in New York tomorrow for some meetings and happen to be free over lunch. Care to meet?'

'Yes, that would be nice,' I said. 'How about Petrossian at one o'clock?'

'Terrific,' Nate replied. 'Am looking forward to meeting you. If even ten per cent of Nigel's accolades are true, we'll have a lot to discuss.'

'Thank you, same here,' I said. 'See you tomorrow at one.'

Nate was already seated at the table when I arrived at the restaurant the following day at ten to one. He got up to shake my hand. Even though I remembered Nigel's 'little Nate' moniker, I was still surprised to see such a diminutive man, short and nondescript, a little mousy. His appearance did not match his assertive voice and tone on the phone.

We spent the next two hours talking about everything under the sun, from politics to movies, to jazz bars in DC, to who was the greatest soccer player of all time. It was a pleasant lunch, and we never got around to discussing the actual purpose of our meeting – Nigel's collaboration idea. I actually found Nate quite likeable, except when he described his government job. In those moments he puffed himself up, talking about his desk job with tremendous pomp, as if he was developing a cure for cancer or evacuating gravely injured children in war zones.

I was looking forward to my secret litmus test for bureaucrats, which never failed with Washington officials: the more veteran a bureaucrat, the more pronounced his or her sense of entitlement and the higher the degree of expectation of being invited for a meal that they themselves had proposed. The more seasoned and entrenched in their political bubble, the more it went without saying that being invited for lunch or dinner was their God-given right. The rest of us mortals should feel honoured at being allowed to invite these masters of the universe, and we should bask in the glory of their wisdom in the hope that we might, by osmosis, absorb the natural authority that flows from their proximity to power.

Nate did not disappoint. When it was time to ask for the bill, he made no effort whatsoever to reach for his wallet. In fact, when the waiter placed the bill on the table, Nate calmly and unapologetically handed it to me. To him, being invited was the most natural thing in the world. Clearly, I was dealing with a DC pro.

We agreed to meet the following week at the State Department. I had to be in Washington for another meeting, so it was fairly convenient.

I have always marvelled at how apt it is that the State Department is located in a DC neighbourhood called Foggy Bottom. Even though the origin of the name has more to do with industrial fumes and fog of past years, it seems like a perfect idiom for America's foreign ministry. As I strolled towards the main entrance, I had no idea how foggy and how low things would become that day.

I walked up to one of the receptionists, handed her my driver's licence for identification, and mentioned that I had a meeting with Nathan Kleiner. She gave me my visitor badge and asked me to have a seat and wait for someone in Mr Kleiner's office to pick me up. From past experience I knew that I might be waiting for a while, so I pulled out the newspaper.

Thirty minutes later, Nate stood in front of me.

'So sorry, Daniel,' he said, not sounding particularly sorry. 'I was called into a very important meeting with Deputy Assistant Secretary Townser. Apologies for keeping you waiting.'

'No apologies needed,' I replied. 'I have no doubt that the meeting with the Deputy Assistant Secretary was important.'

Nate seemed unsure whether my words were intended sarcastically – the fact alone that this was not obvious to him spoke volumes – so he decided to ignore them.

'Anyhow, I'm all yours now, let's go upstairs,' he said. 'We have a lot to discuss.'

Nate must have greeted more than twenty people on our way up, making sure that he addressed each and every one by name and introduced me to them all. I felt a little naked without the ubiquitous government-issued badge that was hanging around everyone's neck (for the men, proper dress code meant that the badge was in the breast pocket). My sad visitor badge felt like a consolation prize.

We finally reached Nate's small office. He sat in his desk chair and motioned towards one of the two other chairs. Since there were folders and documents on both of them, I hesitated.

'Apologies for the mess,' Nate said, as he cleared one of the chairs. 'It has been crazy around here, and when I get back from my trips I have no time to file this stuff away. My secretary is useless, if you know what I mean. Good help is hard to find these days.'

Even though he was in his mid-thirties, Nate looked like he was in his early twenties, and his condescending complaint seemed idiotic. His secretary must have loved him.

'Give me a moment, Daniel,' he continued. 'Let me see if the Secretary is available. It would be nice for you to say hello.'

He left the office without giving me a chance to tell him that this was not necessary. After five minutes he stepped back into the office and closed the door behind him.

'Sorry, Daniel,' he said with exaggerated disappointment, 'we'll have to organize your handshake with the Secretary another time.'

'Not a problem,' I replied. I was liking Nate less and less by the minute.

'Okay, I don't have too much time,' Nate transitioned a little abruptly. 'Nigel told me about your approach to financial development and your so-called platform. To be perfectly honest with you, if I may be so bold, and I hope you don't mind if I am brutally honest . . .'

'Please do,' I interjected, 'by all means, don't hold back.'

'Thanks,' he continued. 'As I was saying, to be really fully honest and frank with you, this platform of yours, well, frankly speaking, it sounds too good to be true.'

I toyed with a sweet fantasy of getting up and telling him that he was absolutely correct, and that the platform was a figment of my imagination. Frankly speaking, of course. But I decided to stick this one out and see where it would lead me. I had an inkling that, if nothing else, the experience would at least have some fleeting entertainment value.

'Well, Nate,' I said, 'I'm not sure how to respond to that. I haven't yet explained the platform to you, and I don't know what exactly Nigel has told you, so perhaps we can start there.'

'Nigel hasn't told me much, other than that you're a great guy and that I should make time to meet you,' Nate replied.

'If Nigel has not told you much,' I said a little testily, 'then I'm not sure I follow your rather strongly worded scepticism about our platform.'

'Good point,' Nate backtracked. 'My position demands of me to be sceptical. I deal with all kinds of people who tell me that they've invented the next-greatest thing after sliced bread.'

'I never claimed that our platform was the next-greatest thing after sliced bread,' I said, getting increasingly annoyed. 'In fact, I haven't yet said one word about it.'

'Sorry, Daniel, let's start over.' Nate seemed a little uncomfortable.

I spent a few minutes explaining the genesis of the platform to Nate, but didn't make it very far. He seemed distracted and uninterested, and none of his short comments and questions were to the point. I decided to cut my losses.

'Your mind seems to be elsewhere,' I said. 'We can chat about this some other time, perhaps by phone, when you're up for it.'

'No, no, Daniel,' Nate said, 'this is very interesting. It's just that we are in the midst of several major anti-corruption initiatives, and I am racking my brain trying to figure out how to integrate your platform in these projects. Please don't misread my reaction. I love your platform.'

Just like Nate had not had any basis for his initial scepticism about the platform, he had no reason to love it either, since I had barely explained a thing about it. Once again, I was tempted to excuse myself and leave. Before I could say anything, Nate jumped up and left the room.

He returned five minutes later.

'Sorry about that,' he said, again not looking or sounding very sorry. 'I realized that I owed the Secretary an update on something important. I had forgotten all about it. Working too hard, I suppose, putting out fires everywhere. Anyway, where were we? Oh yes, your platform and our anti-corruption initiatives. I have mentioned this as a possibility to the Secretary, and I believe I detected some real interest.'

By now I was certain that I was wasting my time. But there was no good way to leave without seeming terribly rude.

'What do you have in mind?' I asked.

'Well, we're faced with huge challenges because of corruption. We work with Transparency International, we work with NGOs, with the UN, with everyone, but we're not making much headway. At best, we're treading water. Take Africa, for example. Everyone is corrupt, and with the emergence of China, we stand no chance. The Chinese throw around their cash, and the rich are getting richer and richer in Africa.'

'That seems just a tad over-generalized, don't you think?' I asked.

'Generalized, shmeneralized, as you people say,' Nate smirked, clearly impressed by his own ethnic wit.

'You people? Wow, Nate, we've managed to reach some new lows here.'

'Come on, Daniel, don't be so sensitive. I don't know why you people are always so . . . let's say . . . delicate. Of course I didn't mean it that way.'

'Of course not,' I said. 'So tell me, Nate, which way *did* you mean it?'

'Forget it, Daniel,' Nate tried to change the subject. 'Let's focus on how the Chinese have just completely corrupted the governing class in Africa. I know it doesn't sound pretty, but it's the truth, and it has to be said.'

'The "truth" is a pretty big word, Nate,' I said. 'You seem rather stuck in stereotypes – stereotypes on the Chinese, and stereotypes on corruption. Did it ever occur to you that the problem could lie less with corruption that is illegal, and more with corruption that is legal? Something the West, including our dear US, seems to have mastered rather expertly, I might add.'

'Huh?' Nate looked lost. 'What in the world is "legal" corruption? What do you mean?'

'I'll give you an example, if you don't mind,' I said. 'A true story, from the very first political rally I attended at a sports stadium in Nairobi. I was five years old, and my father took me to hear Kenyatta speak on Madaraka Day. Kenyatta was fired up, and was deriding his presumptive political opponent in a steamy speech. But over the years, what stuck with me, more than anything, was that Kenyatta was mocking his opponent for the very traits we would consider virtuous today. Kenyatta looked at the crowd and asked laughingly: "How many farms does my opponent have? One! How many houses? One! How many cars? One! And how many wives does my opponent have? One! Now tell me, my brothers and sisters, if this man cannot take care of himself, then how do you expect him to take care of you?" And the crowd loved it! Do you understand, Nate?'

'Not really,' Nate said with a clueless expression.

'You see, Nate, it's not always about the stereotypical corruption, bribing foreign officials, and all that. Kenyatta saw himself as father of the nation, and the better off he was himself, the more authority he radiated. But where do you think the money for his farms, his houses, and his cars came from?'

'Don't forget the wives,' Nate added with a smirk.

'Yes, the wives, too,' I said, relieved that Nate had reconnected to our conversation. 'These were public funds, and everyone seemed to accept it as Kenyatta's birthright that he should be allowed to help himself. Well, perhaps not everyone. Tom Mboya didn't, and he was assassinated about a year after that Kenyatta speech. But pretty much everyone else thought nothing of it. It was certainly not considered illegal. It was perfectly legal corruption.'

Nate was quiet, and for a brief moment I harboured the illusion that my words had been able to distract him from his obsessive focus on China's corrosion of political ethics in Africa.

'But still, the Chinese . . .' Nate finally said, bursting my bubble.

'Seriously, Nate, what is it with you and the Chinese?' I interrupted him impatiently. 'You seem obsessed with them. We both know China didn't invent corruption in Africa.'

'Maybe not, but they sure took it to a new stratosphere. When the chairman of a Chinese state-owned oil company lands in an African capital, that country's President goes to meet him at the airport. The Chinese executive doesn't even leave his plane. How humiliating is that? It doesn't take a genius to figure out who is paying whom. Who is the slave, and who is the slave-master. Seriously, Daniel, Africa has become China's bitch! China is the new colonial power in Africa. But unlike last time around, the continent is not being carved up by the Europeans. No, my friend, this time it's China *über alle*! And *über alles*, too.'

Nate had worked himself into quite a rage. Little speks of saliva, or perhaps it was foam, were appearing in the corners of his mouth.

'Let's take this down a few notches, Nate,' I said, trying to calm things down. 'I don't agree with your take on China and Africa. We have had decades of failed development, well before the Chinese showed up. Not just ineffective development, but corrupt and corrupting development. Very few functional institutions, no state infrastructures that serve their populations, terrible education and health-care systems, no property rights to speak of, little rule of law. All this results in no social foundation, no social capital. A perfect breeding ground for authoritarianism, and ideal conditions for corruption. Let's face it: the West has failed in its development efforts throughout Africa, but it sure did manage to squeeze blood out of stone when it came to natural resources. There is nothing the Chinese are currently doing that the West hasn't already done before.'

'Okay, okay, you've made your point, let's change the subject,' Nate said with a sigh. 'We've barely spoken a word about our cooperation. Why don't we get back to that? It's why you're here, after all.'

'You're right,' I said. 'But before we do that, I have to confess that I don't fully understand what your group here does. Nigel told me a few things, but I don't really have the full picture. What is your function within the State Department?'

'That's not so easy to explain,' he replied. 'Maybe it would be best for me to illustrate it with an example, draw you a picture, so to speak. Suppose a large American company is interested in selling computers in Vietnam. And suppose this company doesn't really have a good network there, if you forgive the pun, hahaha. It has no good way of navigating the corridors of power, and – perhaps more importantly – no good way of avoiding corruption. You know, bribes, kickbacks, all that good stuff. Well, this company might just get discouraged and walk away, which is something it would probably do in a small place like Bhutan with its seven hundred thousand or so people. Because, well, you know, who cares about a few thousand customers! But our company sure as hell does not want to piss away ninety million potential consumers in a place like Vietnam. Now that is nothing to sneeze at. So the company has to figure it out. Be creative, so to speak. That's where we come in.'

'How so?' I asked, in a meek attempt at breaking up Nate's monologue.

'Well, nobody in the whole world has better global networks, better relationships, than the US government. And nobody in the US government has better global networks than the State Department. And nobody in the State Department has better global networks than our group.'

'I get the point,' I said, hoping to halt Nate's rant before he could complete his cascade and announce that nobody in his group had better global networks than the great Nate Kleiner.

'I'm sure you do,' Nate continued. 'I believe our reputation precedes us. Anyhow, where were we? Oh yes, the Vietnam hypothetical. So this American company contacts us – actually, me, specifically – and asks for help.'

'What kind of help?'

'Well, as I explained, help getting access to those who matter in Vietnam. Those who can dole out the big fat contracts, buy millions of computers, service agreements, and all that. You know, help them make a lot of money. Generally, the government, but not always. We put the company in touch with the right people, get them all set up.'

'And what does the company do for you in return? I didn't realize that the US government provided such exquisite business development services. What does the State Department get out of all this?'

Nate did not answer immediately. He seemed to be mulling over his words.

'That's where things get interesting,' he said after a pause. 'That's where things can go different ways.'

Again, another pause. This time I waited patiently.

'In some cases,' Nate continued, 'we just do this as a favour. Consider it a favour to our best taxpayers, so to speak. But, I have to be honest, those cases are few and far between. Usually, we expect them to fund, or rather to sponsor, some State Department initiative, maybe a USAID technical assistance project or some fancy diaspora initiative, or whatever. All in the spirit of public-private partnerships. And, once in a while, we direct them to a private foundation.'

Nate almost slurred the last sentence, and I was not sure I had heard him correctly.

'Excuse me?' I asked. 'What kind of a private foundation?'

'Oh, you know, it could be anything,' Nate answered. 'The foundation of a donor, or that family foundation the Secretary cares about . . .'

'Excuse me?' I said again. This time I hoped that I had not heard him correctly. 'You direct American companies towards friendly private foundations, even the Secretary's family foundation, in exchange for assistance by the State Department? You can't be serious!'

'Why not? What's wrong with that?' From the way Nate's voice tapered off, he must have realized that he had just made a mistake. 'I never said we direct them there.'

'Yes you did,' I insisted.

'Well, you may have heard it that way,' Nate said. 'But that is most certainly not the spirit in which it was expressed.'

'Just for the sake of argument, what exactly is the spirit in which it was expressed?' I asked, dropping all pretence of civility.

'Why are you being so pissy, Daniel?'

'I am being so pissy, to use your words, because you just gave me this magnificent, sanctimonious sermon about corruption in Africa. You spewed contempt and condescension about those evil neocolonial Chinese, who you claim are exploiting the continent and sullying everyone there with their sleaze. But then you describe to me, in the most cavalier way imaginable, how the State Department of the United States of America, in all its power and glory, directs – yes, directs! – private-sector donors to political allies of the Secretary of State. And to top it off, the icing on a cake that already is pretty damn rich, these donors are also directed to the Secretary's family foundation! And you want to lecture me on corruption?'

Nate was quiet. He leaned back in his chair and looked at the ceiling, both hands behind his neck, avoiding any eye contact with me.

'I'll be on my way, now,' I said, standing up. 'Thanks for your time.'

'Wait, Daniel,' Nate said softly. 'I'd hate to part on such a sour note.'

'It is what it is,' I said, making no attempt at a reconciliation. I wasn't in the mood to exchange pleasantries.

'Look, Daniel, these things happen in every country, even in five-star democracies. Nothing illegal about it. I'm sure we both agree that there's too much money in the political world. I, too, would like to see the system reformed. But until that happens, and things don't look too promising on that front . . . until that happens, we have to make the best of it. Lemonade out of lemons, so to speak. All we're doing is putting the money to its best use. That's all I could have meant with "directing". I think there has been an unfortunate misunderstanding between us.'

'No, Nate, there has not been any misunderstanding. This is not about money in politics, or campaign finance reform, or anything like that. This is about a sense of entitlement, and a sense of impunity. It's about the people serving the public servants, instead of public servants serving the people. In its core, it's about corruption, US-style.'

Nate realized that there was no point in trying to sway me. 'Alright, then, let's agree to disagree.'

'Let's do that,' I said, and left the office.

I looked for the elevators, hoping not to get lost in the hallway or, worse, to end up looping all the way back to Nate's office. The brush with Nate, and the nonchalance with which he had rationalized his compromises, had left a bad taste in my mouth. I remembered an Arabic saying that a Syrian friend liked to use: *min barra rkham u min juwwa sakhkham* – on the outside marble, and on the inside filth.

I had always thought that people like Nate represented a few rotten apples within a generally intact system. But the casual, natural clout and authority that Nate had exhibited so comfortably made me wonder: could it be that the system functioned *because* of the Nates of this world, not despite them. Perhaps these apples were not rotten after all, but just ripe enough to keep things humming. Perfect for politics, essential for power.

A security guard directed me to the main entrance.

Then and there, I vowed never again to be lured by the Foggy Bottom Sirens.

Nigel still owes me that old Macallan.

China Class

Nate and his Sinophobic self kept popping into my mind on a flight to Beijing a few months later. I had been invited to deliver a lecture at a Chinese think tank, and was curious to see how the particular brand of power in Beijing would compare to the manifestations of political entitlement I had grown accustomed to enduring in Washington.

The lecture at the think tank had gone well enough, though it was followed by a lacklustre, stiff meeting with a group of economists. After all the exciting buildup, the day had been a little anticlimactic, even boring, so I was grateful when my friend Zhang called me later that afternoon with an intriguing dinner invitation. Zhang could barely contain his excitement.

'We were invited by the chairman and several of his senior managers to a festive dinner in one of the most expensive restaurants in Beijing,' Zhang said. 'It's a great and rare honour. You should feel flattered.'

'I am looking forward to it. Should I brace myself for copious amounts of Maotai?' I asked.

'No, Daniel. The chairman has a taste for expensive French wines. He likes to display his Bordeaux acumen. If there will be a drinking orgy, it will be with some fancy château. Be ready at seven sharp. I will be waiting for you in the hotel lobby. Remember to bring many business cards.'

The chairman was running one of China's largest and most powerful state-owned enterprises. His reputation for pomp and circumstance preceded him. This was a man who demanded sycophantic adulation from all his employees, and was notoriously vicious when he did not get what he believed he was entitled to. Apparently, he also had a brilliant mind with a very fine nose for making a profit, and was considered untouchable both in China's business world and within the Party. I was looking forward to this dinner and the chance to witness such greatness up close.

I was in the lobby ten minutes before seven, and Zhang was already waiting for me.

'Good evening,' I said. 'With you, Zhang, I feel the need to apologize even when I show up early. You're always there first.'

Zhang laughed. 'It's a habit I developed growing up in the dark sixties, when there was no food. You know, the way the first mouse gets all the cheese.'

The chairman had sent us a driver, who was outside in a long, black Audi – a sign of political power in Beijing.

'Pay attention,' Zhang whispered to me as we got in the car. 'This is the chairman's official car that he uses for Party affairs, not the company limo.'

'Affairs, affairs,' I asked, 'or just affairs?'

'Both,' Zhang replied with a wry smile.

We drove through heavy Beijing traffic for about twenty minutes. At the entrance to the restaurant, four beautiful hostesses greeted us and walked us straight to a private room behind a bulky screen. We entered a large room full of men, who parted sideways immediately, like the Red Sea, and a short, slightly hunched gentleman in his late fifties emerged with an outstretched arm.

'Good evening, Mr Chairman. It's a pleasure to meet you,' I said.

'A pleasure and a great honour,' Zhang added quickly, in what felt like a rebuke for my lack of self-effacement.

'Allow me to introduce you to my team,' the chairman said.

For the next ten minutes, the chairman proceeded to introduce me to sixteen men, all of whom handed me their business cards with a two-handed, subtle bow. I was thankful that Zhang had wisely advised me to bring many business cards of my own.

The enormous, round table had been beautifully set with ornate flower arrangements, and each setting had a printed name card in Chinese and English. I was seated on the chairman's left, and Zhang on his right, as Zhang had predicted when we were in the car. 'In China, left can feel right,' as he put it.

'Do you know anything about wine, Mr Levin?' the chairman asked me, as soon as we were seated. Once again, Zhang had proven that he knew his audience.

'A little,' I said. 'Mainly that I enjoy a good glass from time to time.'

'Well, I am about to give you something to enjoy,' the chairman said, as he took the wine book from the sommelier in a well-synchronized motion.

For the next seven minutes the room fell totally silent as the chairman studied the selection with a deeply concentrated, serious look, interrupted only by an approving smile or a disgusted frown, as he leafed through the pages. The sommelier mirrored each of the chairman's facial expressions with one of his own. Finally, the chairman pointed at one wine, tapping his index finger repeatedly at the spot. The sommelier nodded with enthusiastic approval.

'You are about to experience something extraordinary,' the chairman said. 'A 1982 Château Pétrus. The wine of the gods, or, should I say, the wine of Confucius.'

As if on cue, his entire team laughed. The chairman basked in the adulation for about ten seconds, then raised his left hand. The room fell silent. It felt like dinner with Caligula.

'Eighty-two was a wonderful year, just exquisite,' the chairman said. 'Every sip tastes like ambrosia, like a drop from the heavens. Every time I come here, these sommelier imbeciles try to talk me into the eighty-nine, but they have no idea what they are talking about. Each and every one of them is an ignoramus. They should be paying me, not the other way around.'

The sommelier had remained standing at attention throughout the chairman's soliloquy. Without facing him, the chairman dismissed him with the back of his hand, and the sommelier rushed out of the room to get the wine.

Nobody said a word while we were waiting for the wine. The chairman turned to Zhang.

'I hope you will approve of my wine selection,' he said, looking at Zhang. Evidently, the chairman expected to find a kindred wine-connoisseur spirit in Zhang, maybe because he had studied and lived in the West for many years.

'Actually, Mr Chairman, I don't drink,' Zhang said in a whisper. 'I don't do well when I drink any alcohol at all, as if I am having an allergic reaction.'

No words could describe the contempt in the chairman's eyes, as he turned his back to Zhang. Clearly, a person who could not appreciate good wine was beyond redemption. The entire room fell into an even deeper silence. Finally, the sommelier arrived, clutching the bottle of wine, with three waiters in tow. Each waiter was holding another bottle of wine.

'Aha,' the chairman exclaimed. 'Let the games begin.' The Caligula association seemed not far off the mark.

The sommelier presented the 1982 Château Pétrus to the chairman, who took a long, close look at the bottle, and nodded almost imperceptibly. Immediately, one of the waiters handed the sommelier a serrated knife, which he used to remove the thin foil around the top of the bottle, while turning the bottle gently. The sommelier then inserted the corkscrew into the cork and turned it carefully. As he was pulling the cork out of the bottle, the tension in the room was palpable. Everyone was expecting that popping sound. Then the unimaginable happened: the cork disintegrated! I was bracing myself for a tirade of biblical proportions, but to my great surprise, and to the sommelier's even greater relief, the chairman remained calm and motioned to the sommelier to pour some wine into his glass so that he could try it.

The sommelier did as he was told, trying his best to keep the pieces of cork from falling into the glass. The chairman held up the glass in a great theatrical motion and made the wine swirl for a good minute. He then took a big sip, moving the wine to his right cheek, then his left cheek, and then back to his right cheek. Next was a dramatic head-tilt back until he was staring at the ceiling, followed by a hearty gurgle. Then head straight, another left cheek–right cheek passage for good measure. Finally, he swallowed the wine. And then he closed his eyes.

Everyone was leaning forward, looking at the chairman with great anticipation. Throughout his degustation antics, I expected the chairman to spit the wine right into the sommelier's face. But now that he had swallowed it, I did not know what to expect. The entire scene felt like an out-of-body experience.

Finally, the chairman opened his eyes. To my amazement he was visibly pleased with what he had just tasted. He nodded at the sommelier and made a circle out of his index finger and his thumb. The sommelier's sigh of relief was so heavy that I thought he was going to pass out.

The chairman pointed at me and the four other lucky ones who would enjoy the privilege of drinking this extraordinary wine.

'These five get this wine,' he barked at the sommelier. 'For the others, the Beaujolais. And for Zhang over here,' he added with immeasurable contempt, 'water!'

Only then did I notice that the waiters were holding bottles of a different wine. As they uncorked them, I heard that familiar popping sound, and for a moment I wished that I, too, could have some of that Beaujolais.

Finally, all the glasses were poured, and the chairman stood up. As he raised his glass, Zhang signalled to me that I was expected to stand up with the chairman.

'To our guest of honour,' the chairman said with great pathos. 'May our relationship be as exquisite as this wine!'

Before I could reply and thank him, the rest of the table roared *'Gan bei'* and everyone downed their wine.

'It's a Pétrus,' the chairman said in forced joviality. *'Ban bei* would be more appropriate, just drink half the glass! Barbarians, drinking a Pétrus bottoms up! Anyhow, taste it and tell me what you think. I don't think I have ever tasted anything better.'

I took a sip. Immediately I knew that I was not drinking wine, but vinegar. This bottle had gone bad many, many years ago. It was pure, unadulterated vinegar. Possibly good as a salad dressing, but not to drink. I was in a pickle.

'Well?' the chairman said, giving me an expectant look.

'It is certainly the most interesting wine I have ever tasted,' I replied. The vinegar was burning my throat, and I almost gagged.

The chairman seemed pleased enough with my reaction. 'Indeed, an unusual wine. Unusually great! No other wine can match an eighty-two Pétrus. My dear friend, you are in the company of greatness.'

I was not sure whether the chairman was referring to the wine or to himself. It didn't really matter. My main concern was trying to figure out an elegant and inconspicuous way to avoid drinking more of this great wine and average vinegar. It did not help that the other four minions, whom the chairman had elevated to Pétrus-worthy, were outduelling each other in praising the wine and the chairman's oenological acumen.

The person who ended up saving me was the chairman himself. Without any transition he put down his glass and turned to me with a no-nonsense look.

'Enough of the pleasantries. Let's get down to business. Our friend Zhang here tells me that you have some pretty good contacts in Washington.'

'Who doesn't?' I said in a futile attempt at levity. 'After all, we're talking about Wash . . .'

'I have an urgent request,' the chairman said, cutting me off. 'Our group has identified an American company that we would like to acquire. This company has a technology that we consider superior to anything else on the market. I need to have this company. I just need to have it. Plain and simple.'

'Where's the problem?' I asked.

'The problem is that some people in your government are trying to block us,' the chairman said with visible irritation. 'They don't want a Chinese company, especially a state-owned enterprise, to own a valuable US company. They have created problems for us at two levels. First, I am told that they started a congressional investigation about our business in Iran. And second, they may have this government agency block us.'

'Which government agency?' I asked.

Zhang jumped in. 'It is this committee that filters foreign investments in the US to make sure your national security won't be compromised.' He was obviously familiar with the case.

'Do you mean CFIUS?' I asked.

'What?' the chairman blurted out.

'CFIUS – the Committee on Foreign Investment in the US,' I said.

'Exactly, that's the one,' the chairman said triumphantly, pounding his fist on the table, and scaring the living daylights out of his team. 'Zhang told me you would be able to help us.'

'I did not say that,' I said.

'You will help us,' the chairman stated emphatically, again pounding the table. 'You will.'

Clearly, this was not a person accustomed to a lot of dissent. I was trying to make eye contact with Zhang in a plea for help. But Zhang was looking at his plate. I was on my own.

'Could you please give me some more information?' I asked the chairman.

'It's simple. This American company developed this technology. It owns this technology, the patents and all the rights. We need this technology. That's all there is to it.'

'So why would CFIUS block your acquisition?' I asked.

'They claim that we could be a backdoor to the Chinese military,' the chairman said. 'How stupid is that! If we were really connected to the PLA, we would not need to buy this company. We would just hack its computers and steal its technology.'

He said this without a hint of sarcasm. Technology theft was clearly a perfectly rational and viable business strategy under the right circumstances.

'Are you serious?' I asked.

'Of course,' he deadpanned. 'Hacking and removing the technology would be much cheaper. Much more efficient.'

'Sure. And also much more illegal.' I had spoken faster than I was thinking. This was obviously the wrong crowd with which to split hairs about US law.

'In your country, perhaps,' the chairman said unsmilingly. 'Not here.'

'Be that as it may,' I said, 'the CFIUS review process is tricky. Did your company submit a draft notice before filing the formal one?'

'No, why should we?' the chairman said, raising his voice. 'This entire review is complete bullshit, as you Americans like to say. Complete bullshit! I mean, really, what the hell is that! All this bitching and moaning in Washington about the big bad Chinese coming to rape your country, conquering America.'

'Well . . .' I tried to get a word in.

'Well nothing!' he cut me off. 'This is nothing other than good old China-bashing. Let's not forget, there are far more successful American companies operating in China than Chinese companies operating in the US. Far more! And don't even get me started on the whole Iran thing. Who are you to tell me what I can and cannot do in Iran? To hell with those sanctions! And let's not even mention that corruption law! Remind me, what is it called?'

'The Foreign Corrupt Practices Act,' Zhang replied.

'Exactly, that's the one,' the chairman continued. 'It is the height of hypocrisy. We don't lecture or sanction American oil companies that bribe their way through the Third World, but when a Chinese company wants to do business in any of those places, you come after us? What in the world empowers *you* to tell *us* that we are violating American law outside the US? Are you kidding me?! You and your extraterritorial application of your damn law!'

'The chairman has a point,' Zhang piped up helpfully.

'I most certainly do,' the chairman continued. 'But let's get back to this CFIUS committee. Here is what I need you to do. I understand that the Treasury Secretary is the chairman of CFIUS. I need you to contact him immediately and tell him to approve our acquisition right away.'

'Contact whom?' I asked.

'The Treasury Secretary,' the chairman said, sounding exasperated. 'You must contact him right away and inform him that our transaction is actually in America's national interest. I need the approval by Monday, so that I can inform the IDCPC.'

'I'm afraid it doesn't really work that way,' I said, trying to break the disappointing news as gently as possible. 'Dealing with CFIUS requires a formal process, which . . .'

I did not continue. The chairman stared at me with a look of such disgust that I stopped in mid-sentence.

'Listen,' he said. 'I will say this one more time. I need you to talk to the Treasury Secretary and solve this for us. Now!'

I had had enough. Obviously, it was not possible to reason with this man.

'I don't think so,' I said. 'You can keep repeating your request as many times as you like, but it won't change a thing. This is not the way to get things done in the US. You can listen to me, or not listen to me, I don't really care. But if you want to hear my opinion, and if you would like me to help you, then letting me finish a sentence would be a good start. We might disagree at the end, but shooting the messenger will not get you what you want.'

The room had fallen silent in utter shock. Zhang looked like he was about to faint. For about fifteen seconds, which seemed like fifteen minutes, the chairman stared at me. I actually considered my options in the event he would try to slap me. After all, rumour had it that he tended to hit subordinates whose performance he considered inadequate. To my great surprise his expression suddenly morphed into a huge smile.

'Hahaha, I like this man,' he shouted, placing his hand on my shoulder. 'A man who speaks his mind. I will contact you on something else in the coming days.'

Without any warning, the chairman stood up and pointed at one of his men, who immediately handed him three mobile phones. He then pointed at another man, who raced over to us and stood behind me. For a moment I thought that I was about to be arrested for insulting a senior Chinese official.

'This man will walk you to the car, and the driver will take you to the hotel,' the chairman said. 'Zhang, you're staying here!'

Just like that, my meeting with the chairman had ended. The assistant walked me to the car that was waiting at the entrance to the restaurant. He opened the car door without a word, and closed it without a word after I got in. Only then did I realize that I hadn't had a bite to eat to go with the delicious vinegar.

I had plenty of time to think about this crazy meeting as we were weaving through the night-time traffic. Never had I experienced anything quite like it. Nobody had ever spoken to me that way, and I had no intention of interacting with the chairman ever again. I was convinced that his expression of sympathy at the end was meant facetiously.

We arrived at the hotel. The driver smiled when I thanked him and wished him goodnight. He drove off without a word.

I had just called room service to order some dinner, when my hotel phone rang.

'Good evening, Daniel, this is Zhang. I am downstairs in the lobby.'

'Good evening, Zhang, I wasn't expecting you.'

'I apologize for the unannounced visit,' Zhang said. 'I would be grateful if we could meet for a few minutes.'

'Sure, I'll be there in a moment.' I called room service and cancelled my order. Evidently, dinner was not on the cards that evening.

Zhang was waiting for me in the lobby with a big grin on his face. We sat down and ordered some tea.

'Well, that went very well,' Zhang started. 'The chairman really likes you.'

'Very funny,' I said. 'I know that the meeting was a disaster. Let's just erase it from our memory, shall we?'

'Oh no, Daniel,' Zhang said, suddenly serious. 'He *really* liked you. In fact, he instructed me to discuss with you a very confidential matter in Africa.'

'You're kidding, right? What about my unwillingness to help him with CFIUS?'

'CFIUS can wait,' Zhang said. 'This African venture is far more important to the chairman.'

'Please don't take this the wrong way, Zhang,' I said, 'but after this evening I don't think I am all that keen on a relationship with this gentleman.'

'That would be a grave mistake,' Zhang replied. 'You have to overcome your hurt feelings. Don't get caught up in these minor Chinese imperfections.'

'Minor imperfections?'

'Yes, Daniel, minor imperfections. Or, if you prefer, imperfections with Chinese characteristics,' Zhang added with a smirk.

'I don't think I have ever seen a person treat other people this way,' I said. 'Even "feudal" doesn't quite capture it. I'd have to go back farther in time. More like "biblical". Just surreal.'

'Daniel, you have to realize that these SOE chairmen are modern-day gods in China. They have more power than emperors of past dynasties, and they have even fewer inhibitions about using that power. All for the good of the Party, of course.'

'Of course.'

'So please don't be so sensitive, so thin-skinned, and don't get caught up in your feelings,' Zhang continued. 'Growing up hungry and poor has hardened us in China. We don't begrudge today's masters of the universe, such as the chairman. We don't want to topple them. We only want to emulate them. We want to have what they have. Nobody here cares about reforming the system. Everyone is just looking out for himself, in the hope that one day he, too, can be the chairman. So, can we move on now?'

'Sure,' I said, after a pause. 'But that doesn't really change the fact that I have no interest in working for the chairman.'

'Think of it more as working *with* the chairman,' Zhang said.

'Man, you're smooth,' I said with a smile. 'Okay, tell me what this African venture is all about, and I'll decide then.'

We ordered some tea and sandwiches, and Zhang spent the next hour and a half describing the chairman's plans for Africa. It was, without a doubt, the most fascinating reflection of geopolitical and commercial ambitions I had ever encountered. The chairman had appointed a secret task force that spent two years analysing every

African country with the objective of determining the key national assets and resources in each one, coupled with identifying the decision-makers and the most powerful people in those places. I was mesmerized by Zhang's account. The chairman had instructed his task force not only to identify these African leaders, but also to dig up all the dirt there was to be found on them. Their weaknesses, vanities, mistresses, spending habits – everything. He also wanted to know who controlled public opinion in each country. Media, religious leaders, social trendsetters. And he was very focused on the telecommunications infrastructure. As Zhang put it, if you control the telecommunications grid, then the oil wells and gold mines are child's play. The task force had produced a one-thousand-page report that covered the entire African continent. Each country was allotted five chapters: objectives, strategy, tactics, timeline, tasks. Some of the timelines lasted one year, some ten years, generally depending on how vulnerable the decision-makers in the particular country were, and how easily they could be brought on board with the Chinese cause, or replaced. What Zhang was describing was not a commercial plan. It was a military-style blueprint for a commercial annexation. If Genghis Khan and his sons had been this strategic and deliberate, we would all be speaking Mongolian today.

'Phew,' I said after Zhang had finished. 'I don't know what to say. I have never really seen anything like this. I don't know whether to be impressed or mortified. What does the chairman want from me? I mean, after the CFIUS disaster, I can't imagine he believes I have anything to contribute to this African plan.'

'Please, Daniel, you've really got to get over the CFIUS thing. It was just a test.'

'A test?'

'Yes, a test.'

'A test for what?' I asked.

'The chairman wanted to see whether you would tell him what you believed, or whether you would just tell him what you believed he wanted to hear, like all his other lackeys do. He liked the way you handled the situation. You stood up to him. He appreciated that.'

'He sure has an interesting way of showing his appreciation.'

'Can we please move on, Daniel?' Zhang asked, a little impatiently. 'Let it go. The mere fact that he asked me to share his African plans with you says it all. It is a lot more important than your hurt feelings. The goal is not to become best friends with the chairman. Nobody here has best friends. In fact, nobody here has any friends at all. The goal is to work together on a fascinating project, and to make a lot of money. It's a business relationship, that's all. No room for sentimentalities. Just a business relationship.'

'I get it. A business relationship. With Chinese characteristics.'

Zhang smiled.

'So tell me, Zhang,' I continued. 'How do I fit into these plans?'

'The chairman did his homework on you,' Zhang explained. 'He knows that you grew up in Kenya, that you have excellent relationships in many African countries. He believes you will be an asset to him.'

'But how did he even hear about me?'

'I may have mentioned your name to him,' Zhang said with a smirk. 'In passing, of course.'

'Of course.'

'Anyhow, I have taken up enough of your time,' Zhang said. 'It has been a long day, and an even longer evening. Take your time and think it over.'

'I will, thanks.'

I walked Zhang to the hotel entrance. As he got into his car, he turned and smiled.

'The chairman expects an answer by eight tomorrow morning,' he said, before the driver closed the door and Zhang's car drove off. He did not hear me mumble 'Glad I can take my time'.

Despite my serious reservations about the chairman, I was fascinated by this man. Had I not met him in person and witnessed his cold determination and imperial demeanour, I would not have taken this kind of plan seriously. One person was essentially trying to colonize an entire continent, and with strategic and tactical prowess to boot. I realized that the chairman was inhabiting that thin zone in between brilliance and megalomania. But his plans also entailed the potential for significant infrastructure upgrades in many African countries that were sorely lacking in foreign investment, with the possibility of economic growth and increased employment. I decided to give it a shot.

My hotel phone rang at ten to eight the next morning.

'Good morning, Daniel,' Zhang said. 'I am in the lobby, same place as last night, can you come down please?'

Before I could answer, he hung up.

I went downstairs and found him drinking tea. The waitress was clearing the table, and judging by his breakfast display he must have been here for a while.

'My goodness, Zhang, what time did you get here?'

'Six thirty. I wanted to beat traffic, and had some work to do.'

'Why didn't you let me know? We could have had breakfast together.'

'I did not want to bother you this early. Anyhow, it is just before eight. What is your decision on the matter we discussed?'

'I've decided to give it a shot,' I said.

Without a word Zhang picked up his phone and pressed a key.

'Thank you,' he said standing up.

'Don't you need to let the chairman know?' I asked.

'I just did.'

Zhang must have anticipated my answer and prepared the text message before I had come downstairs. Or perhaps he had prepared two text messages, one for each possible answer.

'Since we are both leaving Beijing today,' Zhang continued, 'let us talk on Wednesday evening. I will be in Hong Kong. Please call me at midnight sharp. I will send you an email with my hotel and room information. Goodbye.'

And just like that, he was gone. The waitress brought me his breakfast bill to sign for. I thought I detected a hint of sarcasm in her smile.

The rest of the day was packed with meetings, and I was too distracted to pay any attention to this matter. I left Beijing late afternoon. On the flight back to New York I started to have second thoughts about my decision to be part of the chairman's African conquest. I worried that I might be sleeping with the Devil. Still, I decided to keep an open mind and wait for the call with Zhang.

On Wednesday morning I received Zhang's email with the hotel name and room number. At noon my time, midnight his time, I called him. He picked up immediately.

'Good evening, Zhang. How are you?'

'I am fine, as I am sure you are, too. Let's get started. We have a lot of ground to cover.'

Zhang was beginning to sound like the chairman's mini-me.

'The first task is very straightforward.' Zhang continued. 'I believe you can get to Finance Minister Bagassa. Is that correct?'

'It is. My friend Ayanda is on very good terms with the minister.'

'Excellent. The chairman would like to send a delegation to meet with Minister Bagassa to discuss several matters. He needs you to arrange this meeting.'

'I need some more information,' I said. 'What is the purpose of the meeting?'

'All I can say at this point is that the chairman has earmarked that country for significant investment, mainly infrastructure. Particularly telecommunications infrastructure, and a few other targets.'

'Why not try meeting the Minister of Telecommunications?' I asked.

'Because he has no power,' Zhang said. 'We need Bagassa.'

'Okay, fine, but I still need some more information, and I need the names of the delegation members, as well as their positions and functions.'

'Very well,' Zhang said. 'Please call me in three hours exactly, and I will have that information for you.'

'There's no rush, Zhang, just call me at your leisure when you have the information.'

'No, Daniel, as a general matter I would prefer it if you called me.'

'Why is that?'

'Well . . . well . . .' Zhang muttered, 'it's just safer that way.'

'Safer in what way?' I insisted. For quite a while already I harboured the suspicion that Zhang was simply too cheap to call me. He always went to great lengths to avoid having to place the call, even a local call. When I was in Beijing, he would never call me from the car and ask me to come downstairs. He would enter the hotel and call me from the lobby on the hotel phone. In most instances, he would simply send me an email with the request to call him at a specific time and number. His behaviour seemed compulsive. The only time he had ever initiated a call was through Skype.

'It's just safer,' Zhang repeated. 'When I place the call, it is easier for them to track it and listen in.'

'I don't think it makes any difference whether you initiate the call or I do. It's all the same, if someone is determined to listen to our conversation. Besides, you are in Hong Kong at the moment, not Beijing. Who do you think will be listening?'

'It doesn't matter, this is not phone call material,' Zhang said. 'Just call me in three hours, please.'

Clearly, Zhang was not going to relent on this. 'Sure, we'll speak in three hours,' I said. 'But that will be three in the morning for you. You can also give me this information tomorrow.'

'Nonsense,' Zhang replied abruptly. 'We Chinese never sleep. Time to work. Talk to you at three.'

I called Zhang at three, as we had agreed. This time the phone rang a few times before he picked up.

'Hello, Daniel,' he said in a sleepy voice. I must have woken him.

'Hi, Zhang. I am really sorry to call at this hour. Why don't we talk in your mor . . .'

'Don't be silly,' Zhang cut me off. 'There's no time like the present. I am wide awake, let's do this. Time to party!'

'As you wish,' I said. 'Do you have the information on the delegation that the chairman is sending to see Minister Bagassa?'

'I do,' Zhang replied. 'I will send you an email right after we hang up. I had a long chat with the chairman. He instructed me to ask you for some information about Bagassa. How well do you know him?'

'Not that well,' I said. 'As I already told you, my most promising avenue to him is through my dear friend Ayanda. Personally, I have met him twice. The first time, we were both on a panel at a World Economic Forum conference. At the time he was a rising star in his country, considered presidential material. He lost out to that other creep, but I suppose becoming finance minister is not too shabby, either.'

'And the second time?' Zhang asked.

'The second time was at the UN General Assembly in New York two years ago. We were both bored to death and decided to break away for dinner. It was a lovely evening.'

'What do you think of him?' Zhang continued to grill me. He was all business.

'I like him. He is pleasant and reasonably honest, certainly for a politician. He even has a sense of humour.'

'I don't care about that,' Zhang said. 'What I care about is whether he is reliable, whether he will honour a commitment. And I care about whether he can be induced.'

'Induced?' I asked.

'Yes, induced,' Zhang replied. 'Is he open-minded about the benefits of Chinese investment in his country? Is he intelligent enough to let us help him help us help him?'

'Actually, Zhang, I am not sure *I'm* intelligent enough to understand what you just said. Bagassa is a good guy. He will receive this delegation graciously and listen attentively to what the chairman's representatives have to say. He is enough of a patriot to do what is best for his country, and enough of a politician to do what is best for himself. And he is smart enough to combine the two. Is there anything else you would like to know?'

No answer.

'Zhang? Are you there?'

No answer.

'Zhang?'

I was about to hang up, when I heard some loud snoring. Not gentle snoring that is hard to distinguish from heavy breathing. No, this was some shrill wheezing and thunderous snorting. I was mesmerized. Zhang had fallen into a deep sleep at some point in the course of the twenty seconds during which I was describing Bagassa. Zhang's Chinese 'no play – all work' bravado had come to a crashing halt. I stayed on the line for a few more minutes, and was about to hang up, when Zhang let out three rapid inhaling splutters, followed by a choking sound.

'That's very helpful, Daniel, thank you,' Zhang said seamlessly.

'Which part?' I asked.

'Everything,' Zhang replied perkily. 'I am pleased that you are so close with the minister, and that he will listen to you.'

'I don't think I said that.'

'Of course you did. And the chairman will be pleased, too.'

'Listen, Zhang, perhaps it would be better to continue this conversation in your morning. You seem to be a little tired, which is hardly surprising given the late hour. Why don't you get some sleep?'

'Nonsense,' Zhang said abrasively. 'We Chinese don't need to sleep. We'll sleep when we're dead. I heard every word of what you said.'

I did not have the heart to tell him that he had probably woken the entire hotel with his snoring. We agreed to talk in the coming days.

The next morning, I received an email from Zhang in which he provided me with detailed information for an eight-person delegation to visit Minister Bagassa. To my surprise, he also informed me of the dates for this visit. Apparently, the chairman had already instructed this team to make travel arrangements for the second half of April, and to meet with Minister Bagassa on 20 April. In the chairman's world his word amounted to an act of creation. The possibility that 20 April might not be convenient for Minister Bagassa was clearly too preposterous to consider. I replied to Zhang with a promise to check with Bagassa.

I called Ayanda. It turned out that Minister Bagassa would not be able to meet this Chinese delegation on 20 April, as he needed to travel to Washington DC for the World Bank/IMF spring meetings. But Bagassa was gracious about hosting these guys and offered them any time during the three days prior to his departure for the US on 18 April, or at any time during four days after his return home on 24 April. I took this as a positive indication of interest on the part of Bagassa and was pleased to inform Zhang accordingly. I decided to call him right away.

'*Wei*,' Zhang picked up.

'I have some good news. I spoke to Ayanda, who checked with Minister Bagassa. The minister will be delighted to receive the chairman's delegation.'

'That is excellent news, Daniel, I knew I could count on you.'

'Just one minor thing, Zhang. The minister has asked to have this meeting either between the fifteenth and the eighteenth of April, or between the twenty-fourth and the twenty-eighth.'

The line fell silent. For a moment, I wondered whether Zhang had fallen asleep again.

'Zhang?' I said gently.

'I heard you, Daniel,' Zhang said coldly. 'I thought I had been very clear about the date. It has to be April twentieth. Fix it!'

'Well, unfortunately the minister has to be in Washington on April twentieth for the World Bank/IMF meetings. But he is happy to meet this delegation and has offered several alternate dates either before or after his US trip.'

'Of course he is happy to meet this delegation, it is the best thing that could happen to his damn country,' Zhang said arrogantly. 'I need you to call this man and order him to cancel his Washington trip. The meeting has to take place on April twentieth. Period.'

'You're kidding, right?'

'Do I sound like I'm kidding?' Zhang asked, raising his voice. 'Does this sound like a joke to you? Does it? Does it, Daniel? This is a disaster.'

At this point, Zhang was screaming. I was in complete shock. I had always known Zhang to be a mild-mannered and courteous person.

'Please Zhang, calm down. What has gotten into you?'

'I will *not* calm down!' Zhang shouted in a high-pitched screech.

'What about Deng's famous "keep a cool head and maintain a low profile", which you so love to quote?'

'The hell with Deng!' Zhang yelled. 'Do you know who you are talking to? Do you? Do you, Daniel?'

'Please Zhang, this is ridiculous. Please compose yourself.'

'Quiet!' Zhang screamed. 'Now you listen to me, Daniel! Do you know who you are dealing with? We are no longer this poor nation of the last decades. No longer a nation of beggars, of widows and orphans. I may have grown up in the sixties eating cardboard because there was nothing else to eat, but these are not the sixties! Do you understand? I am important today! China is important today! I matter! China matters! Did you get that? This is China we are talking about, the only other superpower, and one day soon the only superpower, the new ruling class!'

'Well then, if that's the case, how about showing some class?'

'Enough!' Zhang shouted. 'Joke all you want. We will no longer be disrespected. Those days are over. We are no longer in the Cultural Revolution, when millions of Chinese were starving.'

'Actually, millions of Chinese are still starving.'

'Quiet!' Zhang said, his voice cracking in anger. 'The days of treating us like losers are over. Over, I say! You will respect us! We were the Middle Kingdom, and we are now an Empire again! Do you understand? Do you understand?'

'I don't want to hang up on you, Zhang, but if you don't change your tone, I will have to.'

Zhang's meltdown continued, though the decibel level dropped slightly. 'You will not hang up on me! You will not do that. I'm telling you, you will not do that! Not with me! Do you know who we are? Do you know who I am? You don't seem to grasp the gravity, the severity of the situation, Daniel. If the chairman and I determine that the twentieth of April is the day for our delegation to meet Minister Bagassa, then the twentieth it is. Is that understood?'

At this point, my initial bemusement at his hysterical reaction to what I considered to be a minor scheduling issue had completely faded. By now I was fuming. I realized that Zhang's outrageous reaction had in all likelihood been caused by his own promise to the chairman, probably telling him that I would arrange any date that was convenient for the Chinese delegation. Only, Zhang had forgotten to check with me first.

'I'm sorry, Zhang, but you of all people should know that Minister Bagassa is a senior member of a government in a sovereign state. A state that does not happen to be part of Greater China. There are still a few of them left, as hard as that may be for you to grasp.'

'There's no need to be sarcastic, Daniel.'

'Sarcasm is the only thing that's keeping me from hanging up and never talking to you again, Zhang. What has happened to you? Who are you to tell a minister of another country that he should cancel a trip in order to receive a commercial delegation from Beijing? Seriously, Zhang, where do you get off spewing such nonsense? Minister Bagassa is willing to meet this delegation, and please don't flatter yourself – he didn't agree to this meeting because he is tickled to death by the prospect of a scintillating conversation with the chairman's boys. In fact, meeting a Chinese delegation that is showing up in order to acquire the national crown jewels can be political suicide in his country. The political climate there is not exactly pro-Chinese at the moment. The recent mining deaths didn't help matters.'

'I don't care,' Zhang said, his voice rising again. 'I need this meeting to happen that day. The chairman has planned it that way, and it is our job to make that happen.'

'Your job, perhaps, but certainly not mine. I never promised to abandon reason and rational behaviour for the sake of your chairman's ambitions. This is just silly.'

'No, no, no, no, no!' Zhang shouted.

'That's enough, Zhang! You've got to keep your act together.' I decided to end this conversation. There was just no point in extending this call.

'I'm sorry, Daniel,' Zhang said, 'but this meeting has to happen, exactly as the chairman ordered, and exactly as I promised him. You know how powerful the chairman is. Allegiance to him is like allegiance to the Party. It is not negotiable. It is our religion!'

'Then consider me an atheist. This conversation is over, Zhang. Please do not contact me again until you have rejoined civilized society. Goodbye.'

I hung up without waiting for an answer.

Ayanda called me two days later to inform me that Minister Bagassa had just received a formal request from Zhang for a meeting on 20 April. When the minister's chief of staff informed Zhang that Minister Bagassa would be in the US on that date, Zhang replied that the delegation would still be there, and that he hoped this meeting could still be arranged. Ayanda described how confused everyone in Bagassa's ministry was about this odd request.

'What is it with that guy?' Ayanda asked. 'Bagassa's chief of staff told me that talking to Zhang was like talking to a five-year-old. Zhang didn't like her initial reply, so he just kept asking the same question over and over again, until she would give him the answer he wanted to hear. I mean, what's up with that? He's lucky she didn't just hang up on him.'

'Tell me about it!'

I later found out that the chairman's delegation really did show up on 20 April, and met with the Permanent Secretary of the Ministry. Apparently, the meeting was short and not very productive, but what matters most is that the meeting took place on the date the chairman had decided it should take place.

Soon after, I sent the chairman a short note, informing him with deep regret of my decision to resign from this matter. It turns out that the chairman had been prophetic. Our relationship really did end up being just as exquisite as that 1982 Château Pétrus.

Washington, District of Cabals

I mourned the loss of my friendship with Zhang for a long time. I could not understand how intelligent, rational people like this good friend of mine could turn into cartoonish freaks in their obsessive desire to please their masters, and how these masters turned into the same grotesque brutes when the signals to please their own masters were triggered. And on and on it went, kingdoms within kingdoms, fiefdoms within fiefdoms. Command hierarchies, in which doubt and challenge had no place, which suffocated all independence and creativity, and which belittled compromise and empathy as weakness. It all felt so absurd, so alien, and so far from my own culture. My culture – whatever that was! Perhaps Jacques had it right when he quoted Édouard Herriot: culture is that which remains when we have forgotten everything else.

Jacques once told me that my sense of rootlessness would increase in direct proportion to the number of places in which I felt at home, and that the day I reverted back to my core culture, my core identity, would be both my happiest and my most lonely day.

I was thinking of Jacques – it was his birthday – when my phone rang as I was getting into a taxi in London. It was a 202 area code – Washington DC – but I didn't recognize the number.

'Is this Daniel?'

'It is. Who's speaking, please?'

'This is Bonnie. I am the executive assistant to hyuwin . . .'

'I'm sorry, who?' Her last words had been garbled.

'Bonnie.'

'No, no, I got that part. Whose executive assistant are you, please?'

'Hugh Winder,' she answered impatiently, as if only an ignorant fool wouldn't recognize the great Hugh Winder. 'As I assume you know, he is one of the most senior people on the Vice President's staff.'

I knew who Winder was. He was actually considered fairly competent and pleasant by DC standards, which was not saying much.

'Oh, yes, my apologies,' I said. 'I am aware of who Mr Winder is. What can I do for you?'

'Someone in the Senate mentioned you to Mr Winder, and suggested that he talk to you.'

'Do you know on what matter?' I asked.

'I'm not sure. I might have overheard him mention Iran or China, but I can't say for sure. I can try to find out, if you'd like to know more.'

'Well, that would probably be helpful, thanks.'

'Okay, bye,' Bonnie said and hung up abruptly.

Five minutes later, she called me back.

'Daniel – Bonnie here, from Mr Winder's office. I spoke to him. He would like to discuss both China and Iran with you. He's interested in your views on how we can coax China into helping us isolate Iran, since – as Mr Winder put it – we can't expect much help from Putin. He wants to hear your views on the right people in China, particularly in the Communist Party and the military, and which guys we could work with to achieve that goal. Can you find time to discuss this? It might be helpful if you put together a list of top people in China who could be useful to us.'

'I'm afraid that will turn out to be a very short list,' I said. 'But I'll be happy to meet with Mr Winder.'

'Good. Can you be here later this afternoon?' Bonnie asked.

'I'm afraid not,' I replied. 'I am in London. The soonest I could be in DC is Thursday afternoon.'

'Fine,' she said. 'Let's make it Thursday at four thirty. Come to the Eisenhower Executive Office Building. Enter the gate at 17th Street and State Place, across from New York Avenue. Walk up the steps, and present your passport inside. They'll direct you to Hugh's, I mean Mr Winder's, office. Please be on time. Mr Winder has a tight schedule.'

She hung up before I could say goodbye, let alone express my profound appreciation for the fact that Mr Winder could fit me into his tight schedule for a meeting that he himself had requested.

I arrived on Thursday a few minutes early, just in case there would be a line at the gate. Everything went smoothly, and I knocked at Hugh Winder's door at twenty-five past four.

'Come in,' Bonnie shouted from inside. 'You're early. Leave your phone in the drawer out in the hallway and have a seat. Mr Winder has asked Jeff and Linda, his China and Iran experts, to join you and him in the meeting. They should be here any moment.'

With that, Bonnie turned back to her screen and continued to type. Her body language oozed indifference to the point of hostility. I was enjoying yet another cultural DC highlight moment.

A few minutes later, the door opened and in walked Jeff and Linda, each holding a pad and a pen, and each with the obligatory badge hanging from their neck. Neither one looked older than twenty-five. They introduced themselves.

'Hi, I'm Jeff Langer. I am the person primarily responsible for China policy around here.'

'And I'm Linda Anasa. I handle all matters relating to Iran.'

'Nice to meet you both,' I said.

Jeff leaned forward so that his face was only inches away from mine.

'While we're waiting for Hugh,' he said, 'I'd be curious to hear your thoughts on the upcoming transition in China. What do you think the next Politburo will look like? Who will make it in?'

'I expect to discuss this thoroughly in the meeting with Mr Winder,' I replied. 'Maybe we should keep it for that discussion, which I assume will start any moment now.'

'It'll be a while,' Bonnie said without looking up from her computer. 'He's still in the White House. You might as well make yourself comfortable and get started.'

Bonnie's snippiness, Jeff and Linda's air of self-importance – it all felt like a scene out of *Veep*, minus the humour.

'As I said, Daniel,' Jeff launched back in, his face again almost touching mine, 'I'd like to hear your thoughts on the changes we can expect following the next Party Congress in Beijing. My personal take, if I may be so bold, is that the President will try to stifle dissent in the ranks and enforce Party discipline.'

'Wow, you're really going out on a limb there, Jeff,' I said. I was becoming increasingly irritated at being stuck in this room with three people I had no desire to spend time with, waiting for a meeting I had no particular interest in.

'What do you mean?' Jeff asked.

Before I could answer, Linda jumped in.

'I think Jeff is trying to say that he expects the Chinese President to tighten the reins, circle the wagons, if you will,' she clarified helpfully.

'You see, Daniel,' Jeff said, leaning forward again, 'what we at the White House are trying to figure out is whether the Chinese President is someone we can work with. Is he a man of his word or just a Party guy?'

'Can't he be both?' I asked.

'Come on now, Daniel, puh-leaze!' Jeff said indignantly. 'This is the Communist Party we are talking about. The Communist Party! Allow me to explain a few things to you. You may be unaware of the President's background, of the way his father had been treated by Mao and his henchmen, the way he suffered in the Cultural Revolution. But even if you're ignorant when it comes to all that, what you really should read up on is his relationship with the Shanghai elite. You know, with the Party heads in Shanghai. The Shanghai Clique, as they are called. If you don't understand that, you cannot understand China.'

I had not intended to engage with Jeff, but the patronizing tone with which he lectured me rubbed me the wrong way.

'Yes, Jeff, I know,' I said, 'I also read that long article op-ed piece in last Sunday's *New York Times*, and before that the article in *Foreign Affairs* on the President and his Shanghai roots, and before that article there was that extensive feature piece in the *Economist*.

Yes, I read all that, too. They're all recycling each other. Same platitudes, same conventional wisdom. None of the authors met with the Chinese President or even interviewed key people around him. The closest they got is some renegade Chinese publisher in Hong Kong. None of this is news. Tell me, Jeff, do you always regurgitate things you've just read, or do you have any thoughts of your own?'

The room fell silent. The only sound came from Bonnie's typing.

Linda was staring at the window, and Jeff leaned back. The magic of our cheek-to-cheek intimacy seemed to have dissipated.

'So sorry, Daniel,' he finally said in a friendly, almost submissive tone, 'I was not trying to lecture you. I apologize if I offended you.'

'No offence taken, and no apology needed,' I said. 'It had been my expectation for today's meeting that we would discuss aspects that go a little beyond what is conventionally offered up and then reheated over and over and over again.'

Suddenly, the door swung open, and in waltzed Hugh Winder.

'I am so sorry to keep you waiting, Daniel,' he said jovially. 'I was stuck in the Oval Office in a meeting that lasted longer than planned. I see you've already met Jeff and Linda. They're my best people, I'm sure you've had a lovely and lively discussion.'

'Very lively,' I said, as we shook hands.

'Let's get started,' Winder said, as he opened the door to his office. 'Bonnie, please don't interrupt us unless it's the President. Anything to drink, Daniel?'

'I'm fine, thanks.'

We walked into his office and sat down. Winder looked through some documents on his desk, and then left the room again to speak with Bonnie. He came back a minute later and sat down.

'Sorry about that, Daniel, an urgent issue with Jerusalem. What a pain in the ass! Anyhow, let's get started. The reason I asked for this meeting is that I would like to pick your brains on China. Specifically, its relationship with Iran. As you know, we're trying to isolate Iran, with sanctions and all that. We have written off Putin. We know he won't support us. In fact, he will go out of his way to undermine us. Do you agree?'

'Pretty much,' I said. 'Putin has never gotten over the NATO enlargement in Eastern Europe, which he considers Russia's zone of influence. He never will. He curses it when he goes to bed at night, he curses it in his dreams, and he curses it when he wakes up in the morning. He will never align Russia's positions with our interests. Not in Iran, and not anywhere else.'

'Agreed,' Winder said matter-of-factly. 'We're on the same page. What we're trying to do is to get China on our side. Trying to coax them into seeing the Iranian threat our way. You know China pretty well. How do you like our chances?'

'I don't think you can just isolate the Iran issue and convince China to adopt our view,' I replied after a short pause. 'Why should they see it our way? Iran is no threat to China, it's a source of relatively inexpensive crude, especially taking shorter transportation routes into account when compared to African oil. Iran is also a large market for China's manufacturing industry, and even with embargos on money transfers, the oil-for-goods or oil-for-refined-products barters function very well. Sometimes, there are three-party trades, involving, for example, electricity for the United Arab Emirates. All this works in China's favour, and since it doesn't have any beef with Iran, I don't think you can bring China on our side, if you deal with Iran in a vacuum. If anything, you will push China and Russia closer together.'

'So how do you think we could get China to stand with us on Iran?' Winder asked.

'I don't know if it's possible,' I said. 'Keep in mind that Chinese companies, including some of the largest state-owned enterprises, are massively pissed off at the sanctions. Senior officials find themselves blacklisted for buying oil in Iran or selling cell phones or servers to Teheran. For the Chinese, it's just business, and they get very irritated when business is bad. Nobody likes to see his name on a US government blacklist like a common criminal, especially when he's just carrying out his government's policies.'

'So, are you saying there's no way?' Winder asked. He had listened attentively, which was more than could be said for Jeff and Linda, who were checking their cell phones. Apparently, they did not have to leave their toys in the hallway drawer.

'If it can be done, then only as part of a much larger arrangement with China,' I answered Winder. 'We need to make the cake bigger, so that it will be easier to win some and lose some. Without that, I don't see how any side can agree to a compromise without looking like a sucker. So we have to come up with an arrangement where we line up our own national interests and China's interests, and then do two things: focus on the interests we have in common, and ignore the ones we don't.'

'For example?' Winder asked.

'For example, North Korea,' I replied. 'China cares about North Korea a lot more than we do. They also want it to be stable, and they dislike that crazy dictator as much as we do. The North Korean nuclear tests are actually quite close to the Chinese border, and if the shit ever hits the fan, pardon my language, China would be facing an unmitigated disaster. Millions and millions of impoverished, malnourished refugees pouring across the border. China wants stability in the Korean peninsula far worse than we do. I can tell you from personal discussions with senior military guys in China that some of their think tanks have been running hypotheticals on what they could get from us in return for taking out that wacko Kim. And I can assure you that nobody would dare run such hypotheticals if the President had not authorized them and was not eager to hear their conclusions.'

'That's interesting, I've never heard that,' Winder said. 'What do you think China would want from us in return?'

'Well, for starters, they would want to be sure that US troops would not fill the vacuum in North Korea, the way we filled it in Eastern Europe after the Soviet collapse. But as I said with respect to Iran, you can't isolate an issue and expect to have a broad enough common denominator with China. We have to align several shared interests for this to work.'

'Like what?'

'Take the South China Sea, for example. Are we really going to engage with China militarily if the hostilities with Japan escalate over those uninhabitable rocks? Would we be willing to revisit our friendship treaty with Japan, if we conclude that Japan has been acting as an aggressor here? Or, if you believe the friendship treaty with Japan is too sensitive, take Taiwan.'

'What about Taiwan?'

'China views Taiwan as part of China, and would probably be willing to agree to a Hong Kong-style solution to the problem. Again, it's not about North Korea, or Taiwan, or the South China Sea, or Iran alone. It's about creating a large scale and placing the items each country cares about on the two sides of the scale, until they balance out. Basically, what we'd expect from skilful diplomacy – political and military diplomacy. We haven't been very good at it, because we're still drunk from our Cold War victory celebrations. If we found a way to engage behind the scenes, not on official tracks, but carefully and discreetly, with plausible deniability, and put all these issues on the table, then, yes, I think the Chinese would be willing to engage on Iran. At the end of the day, they care about Iran a lot less than they do about any one of these other issues I mentioned.'

'I hear you, Daniel, but some of these issues are complete non-starters,' Winder said. 'Imagine bringing the friendship treaty with Japan to the floor of the Senate. Those guys would blow their tops. Or Taiwan! Forget it, not gonna happen.'

'Perhaps,' I said. 'But tell me, if we're unwilling to put any of these things on the table, then why do we expect the Chinese to sacrifice their own interests? Especially considering that most of these issues, for example Taiwan or the South China Sea, don't affect our vital national interests. Why should China help us out on Iran?'

'Because China wants to have a good relationship with us?' Jeff piped in helpfully.

'China is a superpower,' I said, looking at Jeff. 'I know it doesn't like to call itself a superpower, but the whole world knows that it is just that, a superpower. Its economy will be larger than ours in absolute terms within just a few years, it has a dominant presence all over the globe, it identifies and secures natural resources as it pleases, its President is planning to invest massively in the Chinese military, and its foreign policy will become more and more assertive. What we have witnessed in the South China Sea is just an appetizer. It's not a G-20 world, and not a G-7, or 5, or 3. It's a G-2 world now. Yes, China wants good relations with us, but not at all costs. China wants to be respected. And for the Chinese, nothing shows respect as convincingly as a good old *quid pro quo.*'

'Thanks, Daniel,' Winder said a little abruptly. 'That was worth thinking about. Tell me, what do you think of their President? Jeff here has prepared an outstanding briefing paper for the White House, highlighting the President's family, how it suffered under Mao, and that Shanghai connection. Excellent paper! We have a few more minutes, and I'd be interested to hear your views.'

'Yes, Jeff did share his thoughts with me while we were waiting,' I said, trying not to make eye contact with Jeff.

'What do you think?' Winder asked.

'Well, with all due respect, I think the primary question going forward is whether the President will be able to consolidate power in the Standing Committee, and, most importantly, whether he will be able to establish the Trinity for himself.'

'The Trinity?' Winder asked. 'What do you mean?'

'The Trinity. You know, the three most important powers in China: the head of the Communist Party, the Presidency, and the Head of the Central Military Commission of the PLA.'

'The PLO?'

'No, the PLA. The People's Liberation Army. It was the only thing Deng Xiaoping cared about. He didn't care about party or government titles. He had zero political vanity. But he did care about power and control, and he knew that he couldn't lead China out of its misery and into the Promised Land of economic growth if he had to worry about the military stabbing him in the back. Control of the

PLA was critical to Deng. And it seems to me that the President understands that. Party leadership and Presidency are a given in today's China, but what really distinguishes him is his understanding of the PLA's power. If he can establish this Trinity, he will be formidable.'

'I understand,' Winder said. 'Do you think he will succeed?'

'He will have to clean house first,' I said. 'There are still far too many senior officers, colonels and up, who owe their careers to his predecessor, and especially his predecessor's predecessor. They will always remain loyal to the old man. If the President wants to succeed, he will have to get rid of them. He will have to be ruthless. Probably through a vicious anti-corruption campaign. He won't run out of targets, given how pervasive graft is in the military.'

'So, you like this guy?' Jeff piped in. 'It seems like you think he could be a reformer, a democrat, someone we could support?'

'I never said that,' I answered, turning to Jeff. 'Like most political battles, this isn't about democracy. It's about power. And if the President prevails, which I believe he will, he will be very powerful.'

'So you *do* like this guy!' Linda jumped in helpfully, not wanting to be left out of the conversation. Winder's glance revealed sheer contempt for Linda.

'It doesn't matter whether Daniel likes him or not, Linda,' Winder said sharply. 'Try to follow.'

Linda was crestfallen.

'Irrespective of whether I like him, he has exhibited strategic and tactical intelligence as well as ruthlessness – the prerequisites of power. He will have his hands full dealing with his enemies in the Party. Personally, I think he will be formidable. Whether a formidable foe or a formidable ally depends on us, too.'

'Just a moment, Daniel,' Winder said, as he stood up and rushed out of the room without an explanation. Jeff, Linda and I sat there in uncomfortable silence. After two minutes, Winder returned.

'I'm afraid I have to head back to the White House, Daniel. Thank you so much for stopping by,' he said, as we shook hands. 'It was *so very* interesting to hear your views. We *must* continue this conversation soon in person or by phone. Please *do* stay in touch.'

And there they were! Those telltale DC signs that someone's usefulness had just been exhausted, and that the relationship would evaporate into thin air. I had been around Washington long enough to recognize the signs – the '*so very* interesting', the 'we *must* continue this conversation soon', and the 'please *do* stay in touch', uttered with just the right amount of emphasis in that sacchariny tone of exaggerated intimacy and familiarity. As I smiled and shook Winder's hand, I was reciting to myself the subtitles of his words – 'I'm not at all interested in what you have to say, Daniel, and I have zero-point-zero interest in staying in touch, as I don't think you will be helpful to me and my career.'

'I need to discuss something with Jeff and Linda,' Winder said. 'Bonnie will see you out. Thanks again for stopping by.'

I left the room and closed the door behind me.

'Don't forget to take your phone out of the cubby,' she said without looking up from her computer screen. Bonnie was as lovely and charming now as she had been before our meeting.

'I won't, thanks.'

'Oh, one more thing,' Bonnie said. 'Mr Winder instructed me to ask you for a written summary of your views on China and its President, preferably by email.'

'Excuse me?'

'Mr Winder would like to have a short summary of your views on the Chinese President. You know, the things you just talked about in your meeting. Okay?'

'No, not okay,' I said, trying hard not to use more colourful language. 'Jeff and Linda were taking copious notes, I'm sure they will produce an outstanding summary for Mr Winder.'

I left the office without another word. Even by DC standards, Bonnie's display of unpleasantness was impressive.

Two weeks later, I was in Beijing to deliver a speech. Back in my hotel room, I decided to test my theory on the true translation of Winder's emphatic encouragement to stay in touch. I sent him an email, referring to our last meeting and his adamant request to stay in touch. I mentioned my interaction that evening with some senior Chinese military officers, and how I would be happy to share some of those discussions with Winder in that follow-up meeting or phone call he had suggested.

I received no reply.

For the Love of Gold

Vitaly once told me that history only remembers those who are strong, not those who are good. Perhaps. But high up on the power pyramids there always was this mammoth, greed-fuelled gap between what people say and how they act. This constant 'do as I say, not as I do' was draining, and at the same time a dangerous blueprint for those seeking to climb to the top of those pyramids themselves – ultimately, a self-fulfilling prophecy. As rational as the instinct for self-advancement and self-enrichment is, so much of this seemed gratuitous, almost beyond the control of those seeking power.

The saddest part about my experience with Hugh Winder was that there was nothing unusual about it. Still, the constant exposure to bad behaviour was taking a toll. Commitments were being broken practically as they were uttered, friendships discarded for no reason other than the absence of immediate usefulness. My thoughts kept wandering back a few years to that incident with Nick and Richard in Zurich.

It all began with a celebratory dinner at a pleasant Italian restaurant in the old part of town. It was a lovely summer evening, and the three of us were in a buoyant mood after having reached what seemed to be a breakthrough on a deal that had been tormenting us for quite some time. Nick and Richard were business partners and best friends. They had been working together for so many years that they finished each other's sentences. I enjoyed their company, and was looking forward to getting this deal done, which would also translate into a hefty commission for these guys.

As we were waiting to be seated, Nick's cell phone rang. He went outside to talk, and Richard and I held our spot in the line. After a few minutes Nick came back and handed me his phone.

'Jules is on the line,' he said, covering the phone with his hand. 'He would like to have a few words with you.'

'With me?' I asked. 'What about?'

'I don't know,' Nick said, not without bitterness. 'Apparently, there are some details of our deal that Jules believes I'm incapable of grasping, and he would prefer to discuss them with you.'

Jules was a strange bird, and I preferred to deal with him through Nick and Richard. He had a backhanded way of expressing himself, and I was eager to close this deal so that I would not have him in my life any longer.

'Good evening, Daniel,' Jules said in his nasal voice. 'Are Nick and Richard within earshot?'

'No, they are not. I am outside by myself. Why?'

'Well, as you know, our transaction looks fairly promising at the moment, and I wanted to run something by you, if you don't mind.'

'Sure, what is it?'

'Well, how shall I put this?' Jules started, clearly not very comfortable. 'I know that we met through Nick and Richard, and I certainly appreciate their introduction.'

'Yes, and . . .?' I did not like where this was heading.

'I have discussed this with my partners, and we are of the opinion that there are too many mouths to feed at this table. Your profit and our profit cannot support their commission. We'll treat this as a gracious introduction on their part, and make it up to them on the next deal.'

I couldn't believe what I was hearing. 'What are you saying? Are you asking me to cut my friends out of our deal?'

'Well, that is not how I would put it,' Jules said, his voice a little more subdued than before. 'You are of course free to give them something from your part.'

I was stunned. 'Let me see if I understand you correctly. Nick and Richard put this deal together. They made the connection between both sides. We all signed off on their commission agreement – in fact, it has your signature on it. We have all acknowledged that without them there would be no deal. And now you want to cut them out of it? And you are proposing that on Nick's phone, no less? You can't be serious!'

'I'm sorry you see it that way, Daniel,' Jules said in a defensive tone.

'Tell me, Jules, in what other way would you suggest I see this?'

I was furious. When Jules didn't answer, I added: 'I thought so. Do me a favour, Jules. Please don't ever contact me again.' I hung up without waiting for an answer.

It took me a moment to compose myself. Nick and Richard were already seated at our table. I handed Nick his phone.

Nick could tell that I was not pleased. 'What's wrong?' he asked.

'You won't believe what just happened,' I said. 'Jules asked me to cut you guys out of the deal.'

Both Nick and Richard had a look of sheer disbelief.

'That piece of shit,' Richard shouted. 'Scum of the earth!'

'Incredible,' Nick said, more quietly, 'just incredible.'

'This is why I hate business,' Richard said, a little more composed. 'Money ruins everything. People will sell out their grandmothers for a few pennies. No integrity, no pride.'

'What did you tell him?' Nick asked.

'I told him never to contact me again,' I said.

'Incredible, just incredible. Incredible,' Nick kept repeating in a loop.

'What a huge disappointment,' Richard said. 'Have you ever experienced anything like this, Daniel?'

'Sure,' I said. 'People try to cut others out of their fair share the whole time. In fact, it feels like a major miracle when people act honourably. We once worked with a well-connected person in Angola, with whom we had a success-based arrangement. As soon as the deal closed, we transferred the fee he was due to his bank account. This fellow later told me that in his thirty years in business, I had been the first person to honour my financial commitment to him. He told me that he had had agreements with so many companies, including some of the world's biggest and most profitable ones, but once they got what they were looking for in Angola, they would always forget about their agreements with him. So Jules is just par for the course.'

'But this seems even worse,' Richard insisted. 'I mean, to ask Nick to hand you his cell phone, and then to use that very phone to screw Nick and me! Can it get any lower than that?'

'Much lower,' I said. 'Did I ever tell you guys about our office manager Etta?'

Nick and Richard both shook their heads.

'Let's order,' I said. 'This story will take some time, so we might as well get the chef going.'

We placed our orders, and the waiter brought us a nice bottle of red wine.

'Okay, here's what happened. Etta had been our office manager for many years. She wasn't the easiest person in the world, but she was a hard worker, and I came to appreciate what I thought was her excellent work ethic. Etta came from a difficult background, I believe there had been problems with the father – alcohol may have been involved – and her mother was in poor health. The one thing Etta was not very good at was accounting, and she was at her grumpiest during tax season. In any event, a few years ago, Etta started to behave a little strangely.'

'In what way?' Nick asked.

'Well, it all started one morning when she came into my office and closed the door behind her. She told me that her mother wasn't doing well and required surgery. I expressed to her how sorry I was to hear that, and asked if there was anything she needed. Etta told me that she wasn't comfortable asking, but her mother had no health insurance, and neither she nor her mother could afford the surgery. I asked her how much she needed. And Etta said she was about fifteen thousand dollars short. I gave her a check on the spot, no questions asked.'

I took another sip of wine, and tried to collect my thoughts so that I could convey the full flavour of the crazy Etta saga to Nick and Richard.

'In the weeks following this episode with her mother's surgery, Etta started to behave in a really bizarre way. She called in sick several days in a row and said that she was working from home. She knew that we were up against it in the preparation of our financials for the accountant, but she refused to show up in the office. At first, I attributed this to the stress around her mother's surgery, but eventually it dawned on me that we had a bigger problem. With each passing day, Etta became more and more hostile, and after four weeks I concluded that the situation was no longer tenable. We decided to part ways.'

Our appetizers arrived, and I went quiet until the waiter had placed the plates in front of us and refilled our wine glasses.

'What happened next with Etta?' Nick asked.

'We had a problem,' I continued. 'Etta never returned all the files she had taken home. Our accounting files, and also the bank statements. I had asked her again and again why she needed the bank statements, and she kept answering that she needed them to reconcile the accounts, which made no sense to me.'

'But why was she dealing with the bank statements?' Richard asked. 'Did you give her full authority over your bank accounts?'

'Unfortunately, yes,' I said.

'Are you kidding me?' Richard asked. 'You gave your office manager full authority over your firm's accounts? Signature authority, and all that?'

'I'm afraid so,' I said. 'In hindsight, of course it was a mistake. Huge mistake. But our firm was extremely busy, I was travelling the whole time, and we needed someone to handle payroll, accounting, all that. Etta had always been reliable and loyal, and we had never had a reason to distrust her.'

Nick and Richard were both shaking their heads in disbelief.

'In any event,' I continued, 'this went on for a few more weeks, until it reached a point where we couldn't wait any longer. I called Etta and told her that we would be forced to take legal action if she didn't return all the accounting files and bank statements immediately. The next day a messenger brought us an envelope with some of the files that Etta had taken. I could tell immediately that several pages were missing. Clearly, we had a major problem. Over the coming days we looked into it with some forensic accounting help, and learned that Etta had systematically embezzled a lot of money from our firm.'

'How much?' Richard asked.

'A lot,' I said. 'And what was so shocking was that she had been doing it for years. Hundreds and hundreds of thousands. Her scheme had been so simple: when funds came into our firm's account, she would book only part of that amount in our financial statements, and then transfer the difference from our firm's accounts to her personal account. Sometimes the transfers were small, just a few thousand dollars, and sometimes they were very substantial. The bank never notified us of anything suspicious, because Etta had full signature authority.'

'And some people say that lawyers don't make good managers . . .' Nick said sarcastically.

'I know, I know,' I said. 'It was an extremely expensive lesson for us.'

'I would have killed her,' Richard said. 'Seriously, I would have gone all medieval on her. How did you handle it?'

'I would be lying if I told you that this thought never crossed our minds,' I said with a faint smile. 'But we opted to call the FBI instead.'

'Why the FBI?' Nick asked.

'It's a long story. Basically, the amount of money Etta stole from us, plus some other factors, made the whole affair a federal crime. The FBI agents arrested her at her home.'

'What happened to her?' Richard wanted to know.

'She was sentenced to four years in prison. Her boyfriend actually called me and asked us to drop our charges, told us how sorry she was for what she had done, how she was a changed person, ready to contribute to society, and all that good stuff.'

'Are you serious?' Richard asked.

'Dead serious,' I said. 'Trust me, you couldn't make that shit up.'

'I hope you told the boyfriend to drop dead,' Richard said.

'Only when he added that prison would also be terribly hard on Etta's mother, who needed her daughter after this painful surgery. It reminded me of what a sucker I had been, giving her all this money at the very same time as she was busy emptying our bank accounts.'

'Did you recover any of the money?' Nick asked.

'Very little,' I said with a sigh. 'Our firm's insurance covered a small part, but we got nothing back from Etta. She had spent the money hysterically. Caribbean luxury cruises, one hundred thousand dollars for stereo equipment, a fancy car, even plastic surgery to remove her cellulite. It wasn't pretty. Her spending, I mean.'

Nick and Richard laughed. The main course had arrived, and I hadn't even touched my appetizer.

'Every once in a while, we receive a reminder of the whole episode in the mail. Etta served her time in prison, but she still owes us the money she stole, so the court garnishes part of her wages and sends us periodic cheques for a few hundred dollars. If Etta works for the next six hundred years and we all live that long, we might recover all the money she stole.'

I took a big sip of wine. My stomach was still empty, and the buzz from the wine felt good.

'Anyhow,' I concluded, 'Your man Jules is an amateur compared to Etta. A mediocre Salieri compared to her Mozart genius.'

The rest of the evening was enjoyable, and we let neither klepto-maniac Etta nor sleazy-greedy Jules ruin our mood.

I was back in the office in New York a few days later when my assistant Anna popped her head in and asked if I had a moment.

'Sure,' I said. 'What's up?'

'Everything is fine,' she said. 'There's just a minor issue I would like to bring to your attention.'

'What is it? I could use some good news.'

'Not sure I can deliver that,' Anna said with a serious look. 'It has to do with Jake.'

Jake was one of our senior lawyers. He was smart and efficient, but there was something about him I didn't like. In every situation

Jake seemed to look out for his own interests first, and he never had a good word to say about anyone else at the firm. He seemed bitter that he wasn't a partner, even though he had neither the client relationships nor the billable hours to justify his career expectations. We had always kept our interactions civil, but I knew that he would leave our firm as soon as he found a better opportunity. Jake felt constantly unappreciated and undercompensated.

'What is it?' I asked Anna.

'Well, for the past week, while you were in Switzerland, Jake has been doing something strange. Actually, it has happened before, but too infrequently for me to be sure about it.'

'Please, Anna, get to the point,' I said testily.

'Sure. As you know, our firm has a policy that we get to take a limo home at the firm's expense if we work past eight in the evening.'

'Yes, I know. I instituted the policy.' My mood was taking a precipitous dive from what had been a rather bad place to begin with.

'Of course, sorry,' Anna continued. 'Well, for the past five days, Jake has been leaving the office around five, returning at eight and ordering a limo to go home.'

I sighed. 'Is it possible that he's meeting with clients between five and eight?'

'I checked his diary entries,' Anna answered. 'There are no entries for those hours. In fact, I heard him tell Mark how he likes to go to the gym at that time, and he also mentioned meeting some friends for drinks. If I wasn't certain that he hadn't been working during those hours, I never would have brought this to your attention.'

This was really irritating. Anna handed me Jake's diary entries and the car-service invoices. She was right: Jake hadn't entered any client work past five in the afternoon, and on each day he ordered the limo at five minutes past eight. I was not in the mood for the confrontation I now needed to have with Jake. The limo deal was very clear. We often had to work late into the night. Like many firms, we offered to pay for the car service after hours. But of course the whole point was to make life a little easier for our overworked staff, not to provide an additional perk after a gym workout or happy hour with some pals. Jake lived outside Manhattan, and each limo ride cost us one hundred dollars. Actually, one hundred and thirty, to be precise, since Jake had added a generous tip to the car-service vouchers for our firm to pay. It was another one of his endearing traits – exceedingly generous with someone else's money, and stingy with his own.

I walked down the hallway to Jake's office. He was on the phone but hung up when he saw me. Somehow, Jake always gave me the feeling that he was hiding something. The conversation with Anna didn't do much to dispel my suspicions.

I entered and closed the door behind me. 'Do you have a moment?'

'Of course, come on in. I hope you had a good trip,' Jake said, chipper as can be.

'Let's say it was interesting,' I said. 'Look, Jake, I'm sorry to cut right to the chase. There's something I need to discuss with you, if you don't mind.'

'Sure, what is it?' Jake asked, a little less chipper.

'Well, it has been brought to my attention that for several days you've taken a limo home at the firm's expense, even though you hadn't been working late.'

'Who told you that?' Jake shot back.

'It doesn't matter who told me that. What matters is that I'm giving you the courtesy of an honest conversation, a chance to explain yourself.'

'It was that bitch Leslie, right? It must have been her. She's always had it out for me.' Jake was fuming.

'Please, Jake, stop it,' I said. 'Let's keep this as dignified as possible, considering the circumstances. Besides, Leslie had nothing to do with this. If you don't mind, I would like to know if it's true. Did you take these limos at the firm's expense, even though you didn't work past five on those days?'

Jake did not answer immediately. I had the sense that he was trying to figure out whether he would be able to talk his way out of this. Judging by the transformation of his body language, which went from puffed-out chest to slumped shoulders, he concluded that he had been caught.

'I did,' Jake finally said. 'But there's more to it.'

'Like what?' I asked.

'Like the fact that I've been killing it here. I'm clearly a star, one of the best at this firm, if not *the* best. I left a top Wall Street firm to come here, and yet you guys don't appreciate me, don't recognize all my sacrifices. Offering me a limo home is the least the firm could do for me.'

Jake must have concluded that offence was the best defence, especially when his actions were not defensible.

'If that is how you feel, why didn't you approach us to discuss this openly? Why do this behind our backs? After all, if you are such a star, surely we would do anything to make you happy, right?'

Jake could tell that I was angry. His offence-for-defence strategy hadn't worked out, and he decided to back off.

'I'm sorry, Daniel, I just don't think it's all that outrageous.'

'It's not the amount involved that's outrageous,' I said. 'It's the deception, and your mind-boggling sense of entitlement. You're acting as if this was just some minor misunderstanding, like setting your car's cruise control to sixty in a fifty-miles-an-hour zone.'

'Well, it kind of is,' Jake said.

'No, it's not,' I said.

'What's the big deal, Daniel? It's not like someone has died here. Nobody got hurt.' I could tell from his demeanour that he hadn't quite managed to convince himself with his bravado.

'You're wrong, Jake, our firm got hurt. I got hurt. It's as if you had walked into my office when I was not there, reached into the pocket of my jacket, and taken a few hundred dollars out of my wallet.'

'You are acting like I stole money from you.'

'Tell me, Jake, how is this different from stealing? The limo rides cost money. The money was not yours. It was the firm's. You were not entitled to it. And you didn't just take it, you did it in a deceptive manner, which turned petty theft to fraud.'

'What are you saying?' Jake asked in affected indignation. 'Are you implying that I'm a criminal?'

'No, Jake, I am implying that you're an asshole.'

Two days later, Jake resigned from our firm and took an in-house position with one of our major corporate clients, which led to the end of our relationship not only with Jake but also with this client.

Over the next three months, I shuttled frequently between New York and Zurich for meetings with Nick and Richard. We were working on a major transaction for our firm and were thrilled when the deal closed successfully. We celebrated the happy moment over another wine-infused dinner in Zurich.

Two days later, I received a call from Richard, who wanted to know whether we could get together on a personal matter. Even though I regarded Nick and Richard as a package deal and our interactions had generally been as a threesome, I didn't mind, as I considered Richard a good friend. We agreed to meet at six that afternoon in the lounge of the Baur au Lac, one of Zurich's nicest hotels.

Richard was already there when I arrived, and we spent a few minutes chatting about our children and the challenges of being a parent. Suddenly, Richard turned all serious.

'I need to discuss something with you,' he said with a sullen expression. 'I hope this conversation can stay between you and me.'

'Is everything fine?' I asked. In my mind, I thought Richard was about to break some tragic personal news.

'Well, sort of,' he said. 'As you may have sensed, I'm not all that happy in the partnership with Nick.'

'Actually, I had no idea. I'm sorry to hear that.'

'Well, it is what it is, as you say,' Richard continued. 'I'm getting tired of doing all the work. I've had it! No more being taken for granted by everyone.'

'Who is everyone?' I asked. I wasn't liking the direction this conversation was taking.

'Nick, my wife, my parents, my sisters, even my kids. Everyone.'

'Come on, Richard, you can't be serious. Nick is your best friend. He is loyal to the core. Your kids adore you.'

Richard cut me off. 'Nonsense,' he said with emotion. 'They are all just vultures. I'm sick and tired of slaving away for everyone else.'

'My goodness, Richard, where is all this coming from? Just the other night we had such a lovely dinner. You and Nick seemed as tight as ever. What happened?'

'Nothing happened,' Richard said. 'Except that my eyes have been opened. Anyhow, that is not really what I wanted to discuss with you.'

'It's not?' I asked. 'I'm not sure I want to know what comes next.'

'As you know, Nick and I have a commission arrangement with your firm,' Richard said, glossing over my uneasiness.

'Yes, of course I know. What about it?'

'Well, now that we closed your deal, the moment has come to transfer our commission.'

'I'm aware of that,' I said coldly.

'Well,' Richard continued, 'I would like you to transfer it to me, and let me decide how much I will give Nick.'

I was completely stunned. It all went blank for a moment. Richard had just asked me to help him betray his best friend. Obviously, I must have misheard him.

'I'm sorry, Richard, I must not have heard you correctly. Could you repeat that, please?'

'I said that whatever your firm owes us, I would like you to send it to me, and let me decide how much Nick deserves to get,' Richard said.

'You're kidding, right? Please tell me you're kidding!' I almost shouted.

'Not at all. I'm deadly serious,' Richard answered in a flat tone. 'You met Nick through me, and I have done most of the work on our matter. As I told you, I'm tired of being taken advantage of. No more Mr Nice Guy!'

I still couldn't believe what I was hearing. 'If you really mean what you're saying, then you no longer have to worry about the

Mr Nice Guy moniker. I'm really shocked to hear you speak this way, Richard. I don't know what to say. You are in a partnership with Nick. A fifty-fifty partnership.'

'Well, that partnership is about to end,' Richard said, very matter-of-factly. 'I intend to sell Nick my share in the company.'

'Have you discussed this? Is Nick aware of this?'

'Not yet.'

'Listen, Richard, you and Nick need to work out your situation. I will give you two days to talk to him, and if you don't do it, I will tell him about our conversation.'

Richard seemed genuinely surprised by my reaction.

'I don't understand, Daniel. Why are you concerned about my discussion with Nick? I'm just asking you to honour my request and transfer the money to me.'

'Which part don't you understand?' I asked. 'Nick is my friend, just as I thought you were. Imagine if he had spoken to me behind your back, as you just did, and asked me to screw his partner, as you just did. How would you feel about that?'

'That wouldn't be the same thing,' Richard said.

'Of course it would be the same thing. You and Nick are equal partners in your company, and my arrangement is with your company, not with you or Nick individually. So go ahead and sell your shares back to Nick. I will then honour my agreement with your company by transferring the full amount to him. I'm sure he will be more fair-minded than you and will give you half.'

By the look on Richard's face, he realized that he had just made a bad mistake.

'You wouldn't do that, would you?' he asked.

'No, I wouldn't,' I said. 'I wouldn't do it to you, just as I would never do it to Nick. And I am pretty sure Nick would never do to you what you just tried to do to him. This is just so disappointing.'

'I'm sorry you feel that way,' Richard said testily.

'Tell me, Richard, do you remember that conversation we had a few months ago after Jules tried to screw you and Nick, when I told you about the things our office manager Etta had done?'

'I do. Why?'

'You were so outraged about Jules and Etta, and rightly so,' I said. 'So how in the world can you now ask me to do this to Nick? How?'

'This is different,' Richard said.

'Yes, I know, it's always different. And then it always ends up being the same, doesn't it? *Plus ça change, plus c'est la même chose*, as you like to say. Just imagine if Nick had asked me to do this to you. What would you think of him? And what would you think of me if I actually did what he asked for?'

For a moment, Richard stared at me with a perplexed look, as if my question was just too preposterous to merit any consideration.

'But . . . but that is not what happened,' Richard stuttered nonsensically. 'I mean, really, I never said that. That never happened. I was just trying to make sure it was fair for everyone. For me and Nick. That's all I was doing, right?'

'I have no idea what you just said,' I replied. 'It seems that you are trying to rewrite your own narrative of ten minutes ago. You remind me of that old Soviet joke, when the regime used to have the nasty habit of rewriting history, and one citizen says to another: "The trouble is, you will never know what will happen yesterday." You would have fit right in, Richard.'

Richard had a blank look on his face. I stood up.

'Remember when I told you that Jules was nothing compared to what Etta had done to us?'

Richard nodded faintly.

'Well, congratulations, Richard, you have managed to kick Etta off the top spot of my professional and personal disappointments. You now have the pole position all to yourself.' And without another word, I walked away.

The conversation with Richard kept running through my head. Just like Jake and his Etta-lite exploits, Richard had talked himself into feeling unappreciated and undervalued in order to defend his entitled expectations. Except that, unlike Jake, Richard felt unappreciated and undervalued not just by an employer, but by the entire world, from his family to his business partner Nick, and he used this artificial construct to demand what he otherwise would never have been entitled to. I had witnessed how loyal Nick was to Richard, how he had helped him financially, and how he had supported him as a friend when Richard's marriage had gone through some rocky patches. None of that mattered to Richard. He was a universal victim, and that entitled him to look out for himself only. It would have been less nauseating if he had just emptied their company's coffers, instead of going through all these self-righteous contortions in order to justify what could otherwise not be justified.

I kept my word and waited two days before calling Nick. Not surprisingly, Richard had avoided Nick since our meeting in the Baur au Lac, and Nick was as shocked as I had been by what I told him. I felt awful for Nick. He had not seen this coming at all and was devastated. With one blow, he lost a partner and a friend.

Epilogue

My phone rang just as I was about to step into our children's school for a parent–teacher conference. The number looked vaguely familiar, but I couldn't place it, so I let the call go to voicemail. But before I entered our daughter's classroom, curiosity got the better of me, and I listened to the message.

'Good evening, Daniel. This is Mary Mallacci, Mark Grant's former assistant. I am sorry to call you with some sad news. Mr Grant passed away last night. There is a wake at a funeral home in Manhattan, and a memorial service will take place at a later date. I thought you would want to know, given how closely you had worked with Mr Grant.'

I was stunned. It was a blast from my past. The death of the person to whose hip I had been attached as a young lawyer all those years ago touched me. Perhaps only because a little piece of my own past had just died, too, but I was affected nonetheless.

I had a hard time concentrating on the conversation with our daughter's teacher, and I called Mary back as soon as the meeting was over.

She picked up with a cough. Mary was a heavy smoker, and rarely made it through a conversation without a coughing fit.

'So sorry to bring you such sad news. But I assumed you would want to know,' Mary said, exhaling as she spoke. Cigarettes were clearly still part of her diet.

'Of course, Mary. What happened? He was still a relatively young man.'

'Mr Grant had a brain tumour,' she said. I could hear the sadness in her voice. 'It was discovered just four months ago, and it all went downhill very quickly. They did try radiation and chemo, but gave up quickly. The cancer had already spread throughout his entire body. In the last six weeks, he just worked from home.'

'What do you mean?' I asked incredulously. 'He worked until the end?'

'Of course,' Mary said with a laugh that quickly turned into another coughing fit. 'I'm sure you remember what he was like. He appreciated many things, and he tolerated some people, but his real love was reserved for his work.'

Mary had been devoted to Mark Grant for over thirty years, yet she said those words matter-of-factly, without a trace of sarcasm or bitterness. Maybe she had been around him too long, or maybe she had simply learned to forgive and forget.

'Will there be a memorial service?' I asked. 'Any preferred charity for donations?'

'Actually, there is a wake tomorrow afternoon,' Mary replied. 'The funeral will be private, just his wife and sons and their families. I assume the firm will organize a memorial service for the partners and some clients. Knowing this firm, they will probably do it in a conference room or the lawyers' dining room.'

Again, there was no bitterness or sarcasm in her voice. Mary gave me the address for the wake at a funeral home in downtown Manhattan.

I walked into the funeral home with a heavy heart. I wanted to pay my respects to a man who had taught me a lot and who had, at some point, played an important role in my life. But I didn't feel like seeing former colleagues from the law firm and listening to their unbearably boring war stories.

It turned out that my worries were misplaced. There was not a soul at the wake. Mark was lying in an open casket, his features distorted by the illness.

I sat in the freezing room for two and a half hours, steeped in my thoughts and memories of those intense years at the law firm. I had worked crazy hours, all over the world. The firm even relocated me to Paris in order to get me away from Mark's reach, but we continued to work together during my time in Europe.

I intended to leave the wake as soon as others entered the room, but not a single person showed up. Not his wife, not a son, daughter-in-law, grandchild, not a friend, not a colleague, and not even a client.

The receptionist of the funeral home came to tell me that they were closing for the day. As I was about to leave, a cleaning woman entered the room. She was in her sixties, with an elegant, dignified appearance. She looked at Mark's open casket, and then at me.

'How you doing, sir?' she asked with a heavy Spanish accent.

'I'm fine, thank you. How are you?'

'I'm okay,' she said, looking again at Mark's coffin. 'How sad, right? Only one person is here. Just you. Where's the family?'

'I don't know,' I replied. 'Maybe they were here already.'

'No sir, nobody here today. You are the first one and the last one. I'm closing soon.'

'Well, that is indeed very sad. Nobody else came all day?'

'No, nobody,' she said. 'Are you his son?'

'Oh no, I used to work for him many years ago. I have not seen him or spoken to him in something like eight years.'

'Very sad,' she said with a sigh. 'People go to weddings and to birthday parties, but they don't come to say goodbye to their friends. As if this day is not important.'

I nodded. I was feeling very melancholy and tired, and wanted to get out of there.

'You know, sir,' she continued with a sweet smile, 'my mother, God bless her soul, always say to me when I was little girl in Cuba: two days are most important days in our life: the day we are born, and the day we find out why we are born. To see this poor man lying here alone like this, it made me think of my mother.'

'God bless your mother,' I said. 'She was a wise woman.' And God bless Mark Twain, I thought to myself.

Acknowledgements

I wrote this book on endless flights, in airport lounges, and during long, jet-lagged nights in hotel rooms. Writing it was my entertainment, my distraction, my therapy. Along the way, I was encouraged and buoyed by wonderful people – I owe them all a debt of gratitude.

Thank you, Anita Lowenstein Dent and Tim Corrie, for your enthusiasm and sage counsel, for believing in this book, and for sparing me the experience of having to find and court a literary agent. Without you, this book would not have been published. Plain and simple.

Thank you to all my friends for your superb comments, suggestions, and support: Karin Beck, Ofer Becker, Ian Eisterer, Doris Frick, Jeff Friedmann, Helga Hagen, Oyama Mabandla, Adi Nir, Stefano Quadrio Curzio, Karan Rampal, Randy Spendlove, Carrie Strauch, Enrique Venguer, and Sonja Zwerger.

Thank you to the wonderful team at Penguin Random House: Stefan McGrath for embracing the manuscript and going for it; Josephine Greywoode, my marvellous editor, for showing me when less would be more, and when more would be more; Richard Duguid, for so expertly shepherding the entire process all the way to print; Emma Bal and Rosie Glaisher for your publicity support; Nicola Hill and Ingrid Matts for your marketing efforts; Chantal Noel and the entire rights team for directing the rights rollout; Kate Atley, for achieving the impossible by turning the contract negotiation into a pleasant experience; and everyone else at Penguin Random House who contributed so meaningfully. You have all been fantastic. Thank you, Richard Mason, for your terrific, eagle-eyed copy-editing.

Thank you, Eva and Marc Koralnik, for your thoughtful guidance, and for proving the exception to the curious universe of literary agents.

Acknowledgements

To my parents, Ariella and Zev Levin, thank you for your belief in me, especially as you, Mum, are on the fence about how this book will impact my life.

Finally, thank you, Laura, for enduring the past twenty-one years with me and for remaining my most critical and supportive editor throughout all the craziness, despite having to wonder what exactly it is that I do for a living.

In loving memory of Dr Jacques de Pablo Lacoste (1928–2015)